REPRESENTATION *in the*

AMERICAN REVOLUTION

JAMESTOWN ESSAYS ON REPRESENTATION

General Editor, A. E. Dick Howard

Gordon S. Wood

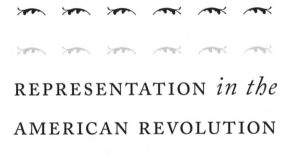

REPRESENTATION *in the*

AMERICAN REVOLUTION

Revised Edition

University of Virginia Press
Charlottesville and London

University of Virginia Press
© 1969, 2008 by the Rector and Visitors of the University of Virginia
All rights reserved
Printed in the United States of America on acid-free paper

First published 2008

1 3 5 7 9 8 6 4 2

LIBRARY OF CONGRESS CATALOGING-IN-PUBLICATION DATA

Wood, Gordon S.
 Representation in the American revolution / Gordon S. Wood. —
Rev. ed.
   p. cm.
 Includes bibliographical references and index.
 ISBN 978-0-8139-2722-0 (pbk. : alk. paper)
 1. Representative government and representation. 2. United States—
Politics and government—1775–1783. I. Title.
 JK54.W66   2008
 320.97309'033—dc22

2008002957

To my graduate students,
past and present

Contents

Preface to the Revised Edition

Nearly forty years ago A. E. dick howard, on behalf of the Jamestown Foundation, asked me to submit a short essay on representation in the American Revolution. As a young professor just starting my career, I found the invitation especially attractive. Not only was I flattered by being asked to join a series that included such distinguished scholars as G. R. Elton, J. R. Pole, Herbert J. Spiro, and William F. Swindler, but I had just completed the manuscript of my book *The Creation of the American Republic, 1776–1787*, which contained much material on the problem of representation that I could draw upon for the essay. I thus was able to write the piece fairly quickly, and the little sixty-six-page paperback pamphlet was published in 1969 by the University Press of Virginia as one of five essays in a series on representation. In 1969 each pamphlet in the series sold for $1.25, or $6.00 for the set. I have no idea how many copies were ever sold or distributed. The pamphlet has long been out of print, but I recently noted that a copy could be purchased on Amazon for $19.95.

The issue of representation in the American Revolution has not attracted much attention in the decades since my pamphlet was published. Since 1970 or so, most academic historians have turned away from political and constitutional history in favor of social and cultural history, especially the history of race and gender. The result for early American history has been a number of rich and valuable studies of slavery and women, but at the cost of relatively little work on issues of early American political and constitutional history. Scholars in law schools, of course, have always remained interested in the constitutional and political issues of the Founding, and a new generation of historians seems poised to investigate once again the perennial problems of how states are established, how constitutions are made, and how the people are represented in government. Recent discussions of the Electoral College and the increasing reliance on ballot initiatives, referendums, and elected judges in many states cry out for historical investigation. And perhaps the postmodern fascination with "representations" of all sorts—the problem of representation, according to one postmodern scholar, being "the inability of a figure to do justice to its object"—will stimulate some students to study the cultural history of the various ways by which we Americans have tried to embody the people in our governments.

This edition of *Representation in the American Revolution* is somewhat larger than the original edition. I have added some new material, especially on the judiciary and representation, and I have tried to clarify some awkward and unclear constructions.

I want to thank Samuel Brenner for helping me transcribe the original essay into computer-friendly form. I could not have begun to revise the essay without his expert assistance.

Gordon S. Wood

REPRESENTATION *in the*

AMERICAN REVOLUTION

Introduction

OF ALL THE CONCEPTIONS OF POLITICAL THEORY underlying the momentous developments of the American revolutionary era, none was more important than that of representation. Nearly all the great debates of the period, beginning with the imperial controversy in the 1760s and ending with the clash over the new Federal Constitution in the 1780s, were ultimately grounded in the problem of representation. Indeed, if representation is defined as the means by which the people participate in government, the fulfillment of a proper representation became the goal and measure of the Revolution itself—"the whole object of the present controversy," as Thomas Jefferson put it in 1776.[1] Representation therefore could not simply be an issue between England and America; it had to be one among Americans themselves. Long after Independence was declared, Americans continued to argue over the ways in which the people should participate in government. In the process, they began fashioning a radically new conception of representation, a conception whose implications were not fully drawn until the formation of the new Federal Constitution.

By 1787–88 many Americans had come to believe that they alone among the peoples of the Western world understood the true principle of representation. Only by profoundly transforming the traditional way in which the people participated in government could Americans explain the conception of federalism; only then could they explain the revolutionary idea that the people were equally represented in two or more parts or levels of government at the same time. Only then was the modern meaning of democracy, indeed the modern conception of politics itself, made meaningful.

Virtual Representation

THE REPRESENTATION OF THE PEOPLE IN GOVERN-
ment had been a troublesome issue throughout much of
the colonial period. But serious discussion of it between
England and the colonies can perhaps best be dated from
Parliament's passage of the Stamp Act in 1765, which lev-
ied a tax on colonial newspapers, documents, playing cards,
and other paper products. Once the English ministry
sensed a stirring of colonial opposition to the Stamp Act,
a group of able English pamphleteers connected with the
government—the most important being Soame Jenyns,
a longtime member of the Board of Trade, and Thomas
Whateley, secretary to George Grenville and the chief
drafter of the Stamp Act—set out to explain and to justify
parliamentary taxation of the colonies.

Before they were done, these British polemicists had re-
vealed the assumptions on which the entire English theory
of politics was based. Their arguments differed; Jenyns, for
example, went so far as to deny the principle of consent as
a basis for taxation. Yet all eventually centered on the point
that the Americans, like all Englishmen who subscribed to

"the principles of our Constitution," were comprehended by acts of Parliament through a system of virtual representation, however "imaginary" and however incomprehensible to "common Sense" this conception of representation may have been.[2] Even though the colonists, like "Nine-Tenths of the People of Britain," did not in fact choose any representatives to the House of Commons, declared Whateley, they were undoubtedly "a Part, and an important Part of the Commons of Great Britain: they are represented in Parliament, in the same Manner as those Inhabitants of Britain are, who have not Voices in Elections."[3]

For the English, election was incidental to the process of representation. People did not actually have to vote for members of Parliament to be represented there. "Copyholders, Leaseholders, and all Men possessed of personal Property only," said Jenyns, "chuse no Representatives; *Manchester, Birmingham,* and many more of our richest and most flourishing trading Towns send no Members to Parliament...; yet are they not Englishmen? or are they not taxed?"[4] The colonists, it seems, were in exactly the same situation as those denied the franchise in England. In fact, declared Whateley, all British subjects were really in the same situation: "None are actually, all are virtually represented; for every Member of Parliament sits in the House, not as Representative of his own Constituents, but as one of that august Assembly by which all the Commons of *Great Britain* are represented."[5]

To most mainstream Englishmen in the mother country these arguments made a great deal of sense. Centuries of history had left Britain with a confusing mixture of sizes and shapes of its electoral districts. Some of the constituencies were large, with thousands of voters, but others were small and more or less in the pocket of a single great landowner. Many of the electoral districts had few voters, and some so-called rotten boroughs like Old Sarum had no inhabitants at all, but nonetheless sent two members to the House of Commons. The town of Dunwich continued to send representatives to Parliament even though it had long since slipped into the North Sea. At the same time, as Whateley pointed out, some of England's largest cities, such as Manchester and Birmingham, which had grown suddenly in the mid-eighteenth century, sent no representatives to Parliament.

What made this conception of virtual representation intelligible, what gave it its force in English thought, was the assumption that the English people, despite great degrees of rank and property, despite even the separation of some by three thousand miles of ocean, were essentially a unitary homogeneous order with a fundamental common interest. Although this assumption that Britons everywhere were one homogeneous people was rapidly losing its relevance in the mid-eighteenth century as the English developed a greater sense of superiority to the several peripheral parts of their empire, British officials nevertheless clung to it as a justification of their rule over the empire.

British officials believed that what affected nonelectors eventually affected electors; what affected the whole affected the parts; and what affected the empire ultimately affected every Englishman or Briton in it. All Englishmen were linked by their heritage, their liberties, and their institutions into a common people that possessed a single transcendent concern. If representation "can travel three hundred Miles, why not three thousand?" asked Jenyns. "If it can jump over Rivers and Mountains, why cannot it sail over the Ocean? If the towns of *Manchester* and *Birmingham,* sending no Representatives to Parliament, are notwithstanding there represented, why are not the cities of *Albany* and *Boston* equally represented in that Assembly? Are they not alike *British* subjects? Are they not *Englishmen*?"[6]

The British justified their hodgepodge of representative districts by claiming that each member of Parliament represented the whole British nation, and not just the particular locality he supposedly came from. As Edmund Burke told his Bristol constituents in 1774, in the most celebrated expression of this assumption in the eighteenth century, Parliament was not "a *congress* of ambassadors from different and hostile interests, which interests each must maintain, as an agent and advocate, against other agents and advocates; but Parliament is a *deliberative* assembly of *one* nation, with *one* interest, that of the whole, where, not local purposes, not local prejudices ought to guide, but the general good, resulting from the general reason of the whole."[7]

The significance of such a conception for the role of the representative, as the great English jurist William Blackstone summarized it, was clear: every member of the House of Commons, "though chosen by one particular district, when elected and returned serves for the whole realm," and was "not bound . . . to consult with, or take the advice, of his constituents."[8] The general interests of the whole people, however much they may hurt a member's particular constituency, said Whateley, "ought to be the great Objects of his Attention, and the only Rules for his Conduct; and to sacrifice these to a partial Advantage in favour of the

Place where he was chosen, would be a Departure from his Duty."⁹

For this reason the older medieval requirement that the members of Parliament, or MPs, reside in the constituencies they represented had long since been ignored, and, of course, such a residency requirement is still not necessary for MPs in Britain today. The representatives were supposed to be independent members free to deliberate and decide by their own consciences what was good for the country, both because a single autonomous public interest was presumed to exist and because the representatives, as the Commons of England, contained all of the people's power and were considered to be the very persons of the people they represented.

With such assumptions it is not surprising then that the English defenders of virtual representation made light of the electoral process by which members were sent to Parliament. Election in and by itself was not what gave the member his representative power. That came ultimately from the mutuality of interests the MP shared with the whole people for whom he spoke. "If it were otherwise," wrote Thomas Whateley, "*Old Sarum* would enjoy Privileges essential to Liberty, which are denied to *Birmingham* and to *Manchester*." Only this concept of virtual representation ultimately justified the binding of the whole people "by the Consent of the Majority of that House, whether their own particular Representatives consented to or opposed the Measures there taken, or whether they had or had not particular Representatives there."¹⁰ However nonsensical we today may regard the notion of virtual representation as it pertained to the Americans in 1765, no better justification of majority rule has ever been made: Why else should we obey laws made by representatives whom we did not vote for?

The Americans, however, immediately and emphatically rejected the British claim that they, like the inhabitants of Manchester and Birmingham, were "*virtually* represented" in the House of Commons, "in the same manner with the nonelectors resident in Great Britain."[11] The idea that members of Parliament spoke for their interests struck them as at once "futile and absurd," contrary to everything they knew about politics: "it cannot surely be consistent with British liberty."[12] The Stamp Act Congress of 1765 summed up the American position at the very beginning of the controversy: "That the people of these colonies are not, and from their local circumstances cannot be, represented in the House of Commons in Great Britain." Through all the adjusting and shifting that took place over the subsequent decade, this basic American position was never shaken.[13]

In rejecting the British claim that Americans were virtually represented in the English House of Commons, however, the colonists never decisively repudiated the conception of virtual representation itself, which held that certain people from the society, if their interests were identical with the rest, could justly speak for the whole. Such a view presumed that electors could comprehend nonelectors when "the interest and circumstance of those who do not vote for representatives, are the same with those that do."[14] In England, wrote Daniel Dulany, the foremost American antagonist in the debate over representation in 1765, a "virtual representation may be reasonably supposed," since the interests of "the nonelectors, the electors, and the representatives are individually the same, to say nothing of the connection among neighbors, friends, and relations. The security of the nonelectors against oppression is that their oppression will fall also upon the electors and the representatives. The one can't be injured and the other indemnified."[15]

As late as 1774–75 some American Whigs were still conceding that virtual representation in Parliament had a relevance in England, where "those who are not freeholders are justly bound by the laws of the land, tho' they have no vote in electing members of Parliament," because all—representatives, electors, and nonelectors—were "governed by the same laws." There was no person in England that did not live in some county that sent several members to the House of Commons, just as there was no person in an American colony, whether he could vote or not, "who is not represented in the provincial legislature where he resides."[16]

A few colonists, like Benjamin Franklin, who were desperately trying to hold the empire together suggested what was commonly called the Scottish solution, that is, the granting of so many seats in the House of Commons to the colonists in the way the Scots had been granted seats in Parliament in the Act of Union of 1707. But such proposals for American representation in Parliament were instantly dismissed by nearly all colonists as "utterly impractical and vain."[17] The Americans objected to parliamentary taxation, they declared, "not because we have no vote in electing members of Parliament, but because we are not, and from our local situation never can be, *represented* there."[18] They knew only too well that even if they should be granted a hundred seats in Parliament that their American members would be swamped by the 558 British members. Many Americans were coming to realize that the problem was not one of their electing or not electing members of Parliament but rather one of a disparity of interests between the mother country and the colonies. The empire, it seemed, was not a single entity after all, and England and America did not share as much of a common interest as many had earlier assumed.

Some colonists, like John Dickinson of Pennsylvania, did see a sufficient connection of commercial interests between the different parts of the empire to justify "the authority of the British parliament to regulate the trade of all her dominions." For without this trade, said Dickinson, England's "strength must decay; her glory vanish," and America's with it. England "cannot suffer without our partaking in her misfortune."[19] But such virtual representation in matters of imperial commerce could not be extended to the colonists' internal affairs. "That any set of men should represent another, detached from them in situation and interest," the colonists said, was totally inconsistent with the principles of British liberty.[20] Perhaps some could virtually represent others from the same society, but surely they could not virtually represent "a whole people."[21] With such statements the colonists were on the verge of declaring themselves a separate nation.

Many Americans in effect turned the conception of virtual representation against the English themselves, arguing that the members of Parliament were "perfect strangers" to Americans, "not bound in interest, duty, or affection" to preserve their liberties, and thus were able "to lay upon us what they would not venture to lay upon their own constituents."[22] By the taxation of American property, said

Richard Henry Lee, English "property would have been exonerated in exact proportion to the burthens they laid on ours."[23] Indeed, the British had violated the very essence of any kind of representation, virtual or not, by framing laws to bind the people, "without, in the same manner, binding the legislators themselves."[24] The Stamp Act of 1765 applied only to the colonists, not to the British on the home island.

Such arguments did not undercut the theory of virtual representation but reinforced it. By conceiving of themselves as a whole people distinct from England, because of the "disparity between the two countries, in respect of situations, numbers, age, abilities and other circumstances," the Americans could renounce parliamentary authority over their internal affairs without necessarily denying the concept of virtual representation itself.[25] And in fact they continued to embrace it even after declaring Independence. As a young Alexander Hamilton pointed out, "the intimate connexion of interest" among electors, nonelectors, and representatives, and not simply the right to vote, was what really made representation viable.[26] This was most obvious in the Americans' denial of the franchise to women and young men. And some such notion of virtual representation, a natural identity of interests between electors and nonelectors, lay behind the various property qualifications for suffrage generally required in the new revolutionary state constitutions drafted in 1776. When some Americans in 1776 objected to these property qualifications and demanded that the franchise be extended to all adult males, the constitution makers were compelled to fall back on reassertions of the doctrine of virtual representation, always emphasizing, of course, as Richard Henry Lee did, the "great difference" between the Americans' case against Britain and "that of the unrepresented in this country."[27]

Moreover, because the conception of virtual representation was inevitably and inextricably bound up with the belief in the homogeneous unity of the people—meaning not only "that the parliament cannot tax the non-voters in England without taxing themselves" but also "that the happiness of the whole nation, must eventually include the happiness of every individual"—the American revolutionaries were necessarily committed to its central premises.[28]

The republicanism they adopted in place of monarchy in 1776 emphasized the res publica, a common devotion to a transcendent public good; thus it logically presumed legislatures in which the various groups in the society would realize "the necessary dependence and connection" each had with the others. "Our situation requires their being firmly united in the same common cause" with "no schism in the body politic."[29] Since the people in each of the republican states were thought to be a single homogeneous entity, they had to be separately represented in distinct houses of representatives in the thirteen state legislatures. "It is in their legislatures," declared a Rhode Islander, echoing John Locke and all good lovers of liberty, "that the members of a commonwealth are united and combined together into one coherent, living body. This is the soul that gives form, life and unity to the commonwealth."[30]

Such legislatures presumed a particular sort of representation—"a house of disinterested men" who "would employ their whole time for the public good."[31] The representatives therefore could not really be "in miniature an exact portrait" of the people, as John Adams advocated; for in the same breath Adams suggested in more traditional terms that the representatives must also be "a few of the most wise and good," who, as the English defenders of virtual representation had implied, would presumably know better than the bulk of the people what was the proper interest of the society.[32] Only men of "great abilities, or considerable property" could produce the knowledge and respect necessary for a representative.[33] But since "great abilities" were difficult to assess, "considerable property" would have to suffice as the criterion of "the most wise and good," which explains the resort to special property qualifications (exceeding those for the suffrage) for the members of the various houses of representatives established in the revolutionary state constitutions in 1776.

The Explicitness of Consent

BY RESORTING TO SPECIAL PROPERTY QUALIFICATIONS for their representatives and by expressing the need for representatives who would devote themselves exclusively to the good of the whole people in each state, Americans demonstrated how firmly they clasped the notion of virtual representation in 1776. Yet even as they hung on to the assumptions behind virtual representation and attempted to work them out in their constitutional documents, they were at the same time caught up in another conception of representation that pulled them in a very different direction and connoted a very contrary notion of the body politic.

The tension had been exposed at the very outset of the imperial controversy. Some Americans in the debate with England had not been satisfied merely to question the claim that the colonists were virtually represented in Parliament but had pushed beyond arguments like those of Daniel Dulany's to challenge the concept of virtual representation itself. "A supposed or implied assent of the people is not an assent to be regarded or depended on," declared a Pennsylvanian in 1774. The people, it seemed obvious to many Americans, "must be represented actually—not 'virtually,'" and not just the colonists but people anywhere.[34] "To what purpose," asked James Otis of Massachusetts, "is it to ring everlasting changes to the colonists on the cases of Manchester, Birmingham and Sheffield, who return no members. If those now so considerable places are not represented, they ought to be."[35]

"Surely," more and more Americans concluded, "he is not my delegate in whose nomination or appointment I have no choice."[36] The popular consent that was so important to the workings of the British constitution seemed, even to those who were willing to grant the relevance of virtual representation in England itself, increasingly equivalent to the people's "actually choosing their own representatives."[37] To be really represented, one had to be able to vote for a representative.

During the debate with Great Britain it had become "plain that the elected are not representatives in their own right, but by virtue of their election." For many Americans the process of voting was not incidental to representation, as it was for the English, but was at the heart of it. Indeed, "representation arises entirely from the free election of the people." Therefore, it was evident that the right of the members of Parliament acquired by their election in England "to pass laws binding upon their electors, does not at the same time give them a right to represent and lay on taxes on those who never invested them with any such power, and by whom they neither were nor could be elected."[38]

In response to the Stamp Act and in an effort to make clear what had been their previous experience with representation in the New World, the Americans found themselves emphasizing the suffrage itself as the basic prerequisite of representation. Apparently, the interests of the individuals in the community were so peculiar, so personal, said one Bostonian in 1765, that "the only ground and reason why any man should be bound by the actions of another who meddles with his concerns is, that he himself choose that other to office."[39]

Such a view could have momentous implications. It was axiomatic by 1776 "that the only moral foundation of government is the consent of the people." But to what extent should that principle of consent be carried? "Shall we say," asked John Adams, "that every individual of the community, old and young, male and female, as well as rich and poor, must consent, expressly, to every act of legislation?"[40]

Once the assumptions lying behind the notion of actual representation were conceded, this conclusion was difficult to resist. And some Americans during the early constitution-making period of 1776 argued vehemently but still sporadically that the suffrage must be extended to at least all adult male members of the society. The growing demand for the right to vote—"the *only privilege* which subjects can *rely* on as a *security* for their *liberty* out of their hands"—was often prompted by the desire to attach as many as possible to the revolutionary movement; but in all cases (as particularly in the arguments against the proposed exclusion of Negroes, Indians, and mulattoes from the suffrage in Massachusetts) it was made possible by the logic of many Americans' commitment against Britain to the actuality of representation.[41]

Even the Tories, as the opponents of resistance were called, tried to throw the implications of the revolutionary notion of actual consent into the faces of the Whigs, the name adopted by the patriots in emulation of the historic English lovers of liberty. The Tories argued that if the Whigs were correct, then no man could be bound by a law unless he had personally voted for a representative.[42] The idea of actual representation had many unanticipated consequences.

Because the future of American political thought lay with this notion of actual representation, in retrospect it is easy, perhaps too easy, to uncover the processes of its development in the colonial period. Right from the beginnings of the settlements in the seventeenth century, the colonists had been continually compelled, by the peculiarity of their circumstances, to believe that the people "should be consulted in the most particular manner that can be imagined."[43] Unlike the jumbled and crazy-quilt representation in the British House of Commons whose origins were lost in the mists of time, the colonists' system of representation had developed in an orderly manner and often within the memory of people. When new towns and new counties were created in the several colonies, they were immediately granted representation in the colonial assemblies equal to the older geographical units; consequently, there were no Dunwichs and Old Sarums and no Manchesters and Birminghams in the colonies. Indeed, when such geographical units were not given distinct and actual representation in the legislature, they might not even be taxed by the legislature. New England colonial assemblies often refrained from taxing towns that had not yet sent their delegates to the legislature.[44] In 1769 when the royal governor denied representation in the Georgia assembly to four new parishes, the legislature pointedly refused to tax them because they were not "particularly represented."[45]

On the eve of the Revolution some colonists had even concluded that such equal and particular representation went beyond mere geographical areas and extended down to individuals themselves—a conclusion that helped to precipitate much of the rural rioting in some of the colonies in the 1760s. By 1776 many Americans were prepared to recognize the principle of numbers as the basis of political representation. Even before Independence four colonies—South Carolina, Pennsylvania, Massachusetts, and New Hampshire—had attempted to bring representation more into line with the changing population of their electoral districts. In fact, by "taking warning from the unequal representation of Britain, by the growth of one part and decrease of another," and by seeking to preserve equal representation "thro' all ages and changes of time,"⁴⁶ five states—New Jersey, Pennsylvania, New York, Vermont, and South Carolina—actually wrote into their revolutionary constitutions of 1776–77 specific plans for periodic adjustments of their representation, so that, as the New York constitution stated, it "shall forever remain proportionate and adequate."⁴⁷

At the very time in the seventeenth and eighteenth centuries that the English conception of virtual representation was hardening, the Americans' ideas about representation were moving in a very different direction, regressing in fact to an older medieval notion of the relationship between constituents and representatives.⁴⁸ While the American experience was re-creating the English medieval practice of attorneys or delegates specifically empowered by counties or towns to vote supplies to the rulers and present grievances from their constituencies, the English, from sometime in the late fifteenth century, had gradually but increasingly regarded their members in the House of Commons less as delegated deputies from particular districts and more as spokesmen for the entire estate of the people.

It is perhaps not an exaggeration to say that these two conceptions of representation passed each other, at least formally, at the time of the American Revolution. In 1774 Parliament finally repealed the decidedly moribund residential requirements for its members and legalized voting by nonresident electors in order to bring the law into line with their conception of virtual representation. At the same time the Americans' new constitutions and governments, in addition to broadening the suffrage and equalizing electoral districts, put a new stress on residential requirements for representatives and electors. All of these measures assumed an actuality of representation and an explicitness of consent alien to official eighteenth-century English thought.

Thus by 1769 the Rev. John Joachim Zubly could confront the official English conception of virtual representation head on. Zubly contended that "every representative in Parliament is not a representative for the whole nation, but only for the particular place for which he hath been chosen...and as the right of sitting depends entirely upon the election, it seems clear to demonstration that no member can represent any but those by whom he hath been elected; if not elected he cannot represent them, and of course not consent to any thing in their behalf."[49] Strong words, with dangerous unforeseen significance; yet Zubly was only drawing out the meaning, implicit if not always explicit, of America's previous experience with the representational process. The revolutionary debates had the effect of clarifying this previous experience and setting representation off in the democratic direction it eventually reached in the next century.

Since ideas about representation were in fact linked with all kinds of conceptions about the structure of the state and the nature of the political process, the clarification was not easy and did not come at once. Behind every differing statement concerning the right of taxation, the force of law, or the sovereignty of the legislative authority lay a varying idea of representation. Because the doctrine of representation was the foundation of all of the Americans' ideas about their relation to government, explaining it was difficult and complicated; changes in the conception of representation required and eventually demanded all sorts of adjustments that were scarcely predicted and often stoutly resisted even by those who held to ideas that made the adjustments necessary. Despite more than a decade of intense inquiry into the nature of representation, American thinking in 1776 had still not sorted out its various aspects but stocked them all in a confused and contradictory fashion.

Democracy in the Mixed Republics

ALTHOUGH, AS RICHARD HENRY LEE CONFESSED, "THE doctrine of representation is a large subject,"[50] open to conflicting and confusing interpretations, revolutionary Americans in 1776 were certain of at least one thing: that "a branch of the legislative power should reside in the people," since as the constitutions of Delaware and Maryland declared, "the right of the people to participate in the legislature is the best security of liberty and the foundation of all free government."[51] That "the Right to legislate is originally in every Member of the Community" all Americans agreed.[52] And happy were the people whose members at large could exercise this right; "but, alas! . . . this equal and perfect system of legislation is seldom to be found in the world, and can only take place in small communities," such as ancient Athens or the eighteenth-century New England towns.[53] Whenever the inhabitants of a state grew numerous, it became "not only inconvenient, but impracticable *for all* to meet in One Assembly."[54]

Out of the impossibility of convening the whole people, it was commonly believed, arose the great English discovery of representation.[55] Through this device of representation—"substituting the few in the room of the many"—the people "in an extensive country" could still express their voice in the making of law and the management of government.[56] "Representation," Americans told themselves over and over again, "is the feet on which a free government stands."[57] Only with the presence of the people, or the democracy, in the constitution could any government remain faithful to the public good. The lower houses of representatives in the new revolutionary state constitutions thus constituted the democratic element in their revolutionary state republics.

This representation of the people, or the democracy, was not, however, to be the only element in the new state governments of 1776. Although it was clear to most Americans that "a free, popular model of government—of the republican kind—may be judged the most friendly to the rights and liberties of the people, and the most conducive to the public welfare," nevertheless, "on account of the infinite diversity of opinions and interests, as well as for other weighty reasons, a government altogether popular, so as to have the decision of cases by assemblies of the body of the people, cannot be thought so eligible."[58] A mixed or balanced government, with democracy being only one element among three, was far more preferable.

The theory of mixed government was as old as the Greeks and had dominated Western political thinking for centuries. It was based on the ancient categorization of forms of government into three ideal types, monarchy, aristocracy, and democracy—a classical scheme derived from the number and character of the ruling power. "There are only Three simple Forms of Government," said John Adams in an oration delivered at Braintree in 1772. When the entire ruling power was entrusted to the discretion of a single person, the government was called a monarchy, or the rule of one. When it was placed in the hands of a "few great, rich, wise Men," the government was an aristocracy, or the rule of the few. And when the whole power of the society was lodged with all the people, the government was termed a democracy, or the rule of the many.[59]

Each of these simple forms possessed a certain quality of excellence: for monarchy, it was order or energy; for aristocracy, it was wisdom; and for democracy, it was honesty or goodness. But the maintenance of these peculiar qualities depended on the forms of government standing fast on the imagined spectrum of power. Yet men being what they were, experience had tragically taught that none of these simple forms of government by itself could remain stable. Left alone, each ran headlong into perversion in the eager search by the rulers, whether one, few, or many, for more power. Monarchy lunged toward its extremity and ended in a cruel despotism. Aristocracy, located midway on the band of power, pulled in both directions and created "faction and multiplied usurpation."[60] Democracy, seeking more power in the hands of the people, degenerated into anarchy and tumult.

The mixed or balanced polity was designed to prevent these perversions. By including each of the classic simple forms of government in the same constitution, political fluctuations would cease. The forces pulling in one direction would be counterbalanced by opposing forces. Monarchy and democracy would each prevent the other from sliding off toward an extremity on the spectrum of power; and to keep the government from oscillating like a pendulum, the aristocracy would act as a centering stabilizer. Only through this reciprocal sharing of political power by the one, the few, and the many could the desirable qualities of each be preserved. As John Adams, who of all the revolutionaries clung longest and most tenaciously to this ancient theory of mixed government, told his Braintree audience, "Liberty depends upon an exact Ballance, a nice Counter-poise of all the Powers of the state....The best Governments of the World have been mixed."[61]

Yet simple as it seems, the theory of mixture was complicated and comprehensive, concerned not merely with the ruling powers of government but as well with the orders or estates of the society expressing themselves in these powers. It was its ability to relate the government to the society, to involve in the government all the social orders of the body politic—the monarch, the nobility, and the people—that made the theory so persuasive. The social or psychological qualities that men used to characterize each particular form of government—"honor, virtue and fear" Virginian Edmund Pendleton described them in 1776— were significant because the mixed government was not an institutional abstraction set apart from the society but was in fact the very embodiment of the society.[62] For Englishmen these three orders of king, lords, and people constituted all their society, and "the meeting of these three estates in Parliament is what we call our government."[63] This marvelous coincidence between the society and the government—the correspondence of the three estates of the realm to the three classic forms of government, monarchy, aristocracy, and democracy—gave the eighteenth-century English constitution its awesomeness and Parliament its sovereignty, or its power to enact whatever it would for the society it fully embodied.[64]

Most Americans in 1776 set about building their new republics within the confines of this theory of mixed government, "not so much from attachment by habit to such a plan of power...," John Adams recalled, "as from conviction that it was founded in nature and reason."[65] "The Constitution of Britain had for its object the union of the three grand qualities of virtue, wisdom, and power as the characteristicks of perfect Government," William Hooper informed the North Carolina congress framing a state constitution in the fall of 1776. "Might not this or something like this serve as a Model for us."[66] A mixed elective republic was as entirely possible as a mixed hereditary monarchy, since independence from England and the elimination of the king had not altered the basic postulates of the science of politics. After all, declared John Adams in 1772, "the republics of Greece, Rome, Carthage were all mixed Governments."[67] And, as the English radical James Burgh had written, this mixture had never been an objection against their being republican.[68] Had not the English classical republicans Milton and Sidney, through the influence of both Polybius and Machiavelli, demonstrated that a republic was superior to a monarchy in realizing the ideal of a mixed state?[69]

In other words, an elective republican system was as capable as a hereditary monarchical system of incorporating the three natural orders existing in any society into a government. Even though the republican governors and upper houses in the several states were now to be periodically selected by the people, no one clearly foresaw in 1776 that their essential nature was thereby to be changed. The monarchical element might be present in a mixed constitution without there being any king, just as the aristocratic element might be present without there being any legally defined nobility. Any properly balanced republic required the incorporating into the government of these two social orders along with, of course, the democratic element, or the people themselves, represented in the various houses of representatives.

Whether Americans in 1776 clearly realized it or not, this theory of a mixed republic rested upon the English conception of virtual representation. Only by conceiving of the people as a homogeneous order tied to their representatives in the legislature by bonds of mutual interest could the various parts of the mixed state be thought to embody different social orders. The electoral process and the suffrage could never be the means and measure of representation; otherwise, no intelligible distinction among similarly elected governors, senators, and representatives could be maintained. Although it was now clear that all parts of the republican governments derived their ultimate authority from the people, this common derivation of authority was not the same as representation, nor did it make the several branches of the government alike. The people, although now responsible for selecting all parts of the mixed republics, were still thought to be represented exclusively in the lower houses of the legislatures. The elected governors embodied "the one" in the society and the elected senators "the few"; although elected, neither governors nor senates had constituents in the way the houses of representatives did.

But American experience eventually made sustaining

the notion of virtual representation impossible. The mutuality of interests between representatives and constituents that lay at the heart of virtual representation, a mutuality of interests that had never been strong in America to begin with, was now eroded by the most corrosive kinds of politics and polemics. Many Americans soon began to recognize during the crisis of Independence and in the years following that they could not maintain their concept of mixed government inviolate and at the same time do justice to their developing ideas of actual representation. It became increasingly evident that the people of each state were not homogeneous entities capable of being represented by empathic elites. Everywhere politicians and writers put more and more emphasis on the explicitness of consent: on equal electoral districts, on a broadened suffrage, on residence requirements for both the elected and the electors, on the strict accountability of representatives to the local electorate, indeed, on the closest possible ties between members and their particular constituents. This stress on the actuality of representation and the consequent weakening of the idea of virtual representation demanded a readjustment in people's thinking about the concept of mixed government, a readjustment that eventually led to a new and radical reconstruction of political theory.

The Disintegration of Representation

JUST AS THE CHARACTERISTICS OF VIRTUAL REPRESEN-
tation were trust and mutuality of interests between representatives and constituents, so the characteristics of actual representation were mistrust and even an antagonism
of interest between members and constituents. Indeed, as
one Whig noted in 1774, the conception of virtual representation, with its assumption that the representatives were
in truth the entire people, presumed a more representative legislature, a closer identity between constituents and
members, than did the belief that the representatives were
only agents, or as Josiah Tucker, the cantankerous dean of
Gloucester, snorted, "mere Attornies of those who elected
them" who "ought to do as they are bid," and who "ought
not to prefer their own private opinions to the judgments
of their constituents."[70] Indeed, it was this breakdown in
the sense of mutuality of interests, this mistrust of the
representational process, that made actual representation
meaningful.

Since actual representation was based on the people's
mistrust of those they elected, Americans tended to push

for the most explicit and broadest kind of consent, which generally meant voting. The mutuality of interests that made virtual representation meaningful in England was in America so weak and tenuous that the representatives could not be trusted to speak for the interests of their constituents unless they actually voted for them. Actual representation thus made the process of election not incidental but central to representation. Actual representation became the key to the peculiarities of American constitutionalism and government. People wanted elected officials that were like them in every way, not only in ideas but in religion, ethnicity, or social class. Already Americans were expressing the idea that the elected representatives had to be not only *for* the people but also *of* the people.

During the revolutionary crisis artisans or mechanics in particular developed a heightened sense of their collective identity, and they began speaking openly of a distinct "mechanical interest" in the society. But the newly aroused craftsmen and protobusinessmen were not content simply to be a pressure group. They wanted to make governmental decisions for themselves, and they now called for explicit representation of their interests in government.

By the 1770s artisans in the various port cities were forming slates of candidates and were being elected as artisans to various committees and congresses and other prominent offices. The traditional gentry no longer seemed capable of speaking for the interests of artisans or of any other groups of ordinary people. "If ever therefore your rights are preserved," the mechanics told each other, "it must be through the virtue and integrity of the middling sort, as farmers, tradesmen, etc. who despise venality, and best know the sweets of liberty." Artisans, they said, could trust in government only spokesmen of their own kind, only those "from whose Principles," as South Carolina craftsmen declared, they had reason "to expect the greatest assistances."[71]

In 1770 artisans in Philadelphia won four of the ten elected city offices. In the wake of their success, other particular interests—religious and ethnic groups—clamored for equal recognition through representation in government. By 1774 the Philadelphia Committee of Nineteen, the principal organization of the resistance movement, invited six persons from each religious association in the city to take part in its deliberations. In June 1774 the proposal of the Philadelphia radicals to add seven mechanics and six Germans to the committee that would succeed the Nineteen marked a significant moment in the history of American politics. It was the beginning of what would eventually become the very stuff of American politics—a consciously pluralistic, interest-group brand of politics. By 1775 the royal governor of Georgia could only shake his head in astonishment that the revolutionary committee in control of Savannah consisted of "a Parcel of the Lowest People, chiefly carpenters, shoemakers, blacksmiths etc. with a Jew at their head."[72]

Such popular and pluralist representation was only the fulfillment of the localist tendencies of public life that went back to the seventeenth-century beginnings of American history. People increasingly felt so disconnected from one another and so self-conscious of their distinct interests that they could not trust anyone different or far removed from themselves to speak for them in government. American democracy grew out of this pervasive mistrust.

Such popular pluralistic representation was momentous enough by itself. What made it doubly so was that these demands for interest-group representation were accompanied by a full-scale ideological defense of self-interest in the making of laws. As early as the 1760s groups of New York artisans were willing to say bluntly and publicly in justification of their desire for explicit representation in government that "Self-Interest is the grand Principle of all Human Actions," and that "it is unreasonable and vain to expect Service from a Man who must act contrary to his own Interests to perform it." Every man in the society had interests, not just noblemen and gentlemen, and therefore every man in the society had the right to hold office in government. "Every Man who honestly supports a Family by useful Employment," the New York radicals argued, "is honourable enough for any office in the State, that his abilities are equal to. And in the great essential Interests of a Nation, which are so plain that every one may understand them,—as every individual is interested, all have an equal Right to declare their Interests, and to have them regarded."[73]

When artisans and other interested men in the 1760s and 1770s defended their self-interestedness and claimed that they and their marketplace interests had a right to be particularly represented in government, they were in effect demanding to be judges in their own causes; they were insisting that party or faction be made a legitimate participant in government. This was tantamount to saying that the object of government was the pursuit of private interests instead of the public good. Such ideas ran too strongly against the grain of enlightened republican thinking to be widely acceptable as yet.

Nevertheless, these early demands for participation in government by artisans and other ordinary workers were sufficiently novel and threatening to provoke responses from the gentry leaders. However respectful of the people such revolutionary leaders might have been, they were not prepared to accept the participatory representation in government of carpenters, butchers, and shoemakers, even when they were wealthy protobusinessmen with many employees.

It was inconceivable to someone like the Oxford-educated William Henry Drayton of South Carolina that gentlemen with a liberal education who had read a little should have to consult on the difficulties of government "with men who never were in a way to study, or to advise upon any points, but rules how to cut up a beast in the market to the best advantage, to cobble an old shoe in the neatest manner, or to build a necessary house." Drayton was willing to admit that "the *profanum vulgus*" was "a species of mankind," even that mechanics were "a useful and necessary part of society," but, he said with more courage than discretion, such men were not meant to govern. "Nature never intended that such men should be profound politicians or able statesmen. . . . Will a man in his right senses," he asked, "be directed by an illiterate person in the prosecution of a law-suit? Or, when a ship is in a storm, and near the rocks who, but a fool, would put the helm into the hand of a landsman?"[74]

It was not, said the gentry, just their lack of ability that disqualified artisans from important governmental office. It was their deep involvement in work, trade, and business, their occupations—their very interestedness—that made them ignoble and thus unfit to be legislative representatives. They lacked the requisite liberal, disinterested, cosmopolitan outlook that presumably was possessed only by enlightened and liberally educated persons—only by gentry superiors who knew better what was good for the whole society.

Yet the mistrust that fed the popular emphasis on actual representation only intensified—perhaps most clearly seen in the expanded ways in which constituents began resorting to instructions in order to better control their delegates in the several state legislatures. The Whigs in Delaware in May 1776 sensed the changes taking place in American ideas about representation, sensed in fact where the revolutionary movement and arguments were going. Desiring to press the Delaware Assembly into declaring Independence, a group of radicals led by Caesar and Thomas Rodney first thought "it was best to present petitions to the Assembly"; but then realizing that "there seems some impropriety in a petition," they "changed the mode into Instructions."[75]

This change of form was actually one of substance, for the petitioning and the instructing of representatives were rapidly becoming symbols of two quite different attitudes toward representation, indeed between virtual and actual representation. Petitioning implied that the representative was a superior so completely possessed of the full authority of all the people that he must be solicited, never commanded, by his particular electors, and must speak only for the general good and not merely for the interests of his local constituents. Instructing, on the other hand, implied that the delegate represented no one but the people who elected him, and that he was simply a mistrusted agent of his electors, bound to follow their directions.

In the years following the Declaration of Independence, more and more constituencies, even those which had no long tradition of instructions, resorted to the issuing of binding directions to their representatives in an effort to anchor what seemed to be drifting legislatures.[76] By the 1780s even in the "Nabob"-dominated state of South Carolina the right of instructing was being called "the most invaluable privilege of a free people." If the doctrine of binding instructions be denied, wrote William Hornby, a brewer and a leading critic of the planter aristocracy, "it will at one stroke transform us into *legal* SLAVES to our *lordly* SERVANTS." Yet, wrote Christopher Gadsden, defending the independence and integrity of the legislature and the "old *friendly* habits" of South Carolina, this "fettering" of the representatives "with absolute instructions" had "a great *tendency* in our circumstances, *not only* at times of hindering and embarrassing public business, but *very probably*, of being the *means* of setting up a *directing* club or committee, in the city or district where the legislature may sit, which may... serve to put the legislature into *leading* strings, and make them as a *body* contemptible, and their members as individuals obsequious to the great men of the club." Unless the members were left "*untrammeled*, to act by their own best judgments, upon any point of importance, after it has undergone a thorough discussion in the house," the legislature would never be able to "attend to the *general combined* interest of *all* the state *put together.*"[77]

But this was not really the way the people should legislate for themselves, wrote an anonymous Carolinian in 1783, in terms that disclosed just how far Americans were willing to carry their concept of actual representation. "Whatever difficulty there may be in convening and taking the sense of all the members of a society at once; there is none in assembling parishes separately." After such deliberation and voting in the separate districts, "a final issue may be taken in General Assembly on a certain majority of vouched and recorded decisions." The representatives were in effect agents elected and controlled by quasi-independent constituencies. If they were otherwise, "if, after election, the members are free to act of their own accord, instead of abiding by the direction of their constituents," then election by districts was meaningless, for "it would be a matter of indifference from what part of a Republic the Legislative body was taken." "What nation in their senses," concluded the writer in a remarkably revealing statement, "ever sent ambassadors to another without limiting them by instructions." In America the representative legislature had become precisely what Edmund Burke said it should never become: "a *congress* of ambassadors from different and hostile interests, which interests each must maintain, as an agent and advocate, against other agents and advocates."[78]

Such a conception of the relation between constituents and representatives could, if carried far enough, transform the body politic, the single homogeneous unity of the people, into an "*infinite number of jarring, disunited factions*."[79] The inhabitants of the towns or districts of a state generally saw "the common interest only through the eyes of their deputies," who in turn proposed "private or particular advantages to their own towns or persons, to the prejudice of other towns and the rest of their fellow subjects." Indeed, perhaps there was no common interest to be found at all: "legislators can only perceive so many different interests in a confused manner."[80]

By the mid-1780s the Reverend Levi Hart, minister of Preston, Connecticut, conceded that the members of the Connecticut General Assembly represented only their respective towns or corporations, "the interest of each corporation is to be regarded individually, as connected with that of the state."[81] The requirement in Pennsylvania that electors be residents of the districts in which they voted, complained one critic in 1786, was turning the counties of the state into "independent hostile republics, with discordant objects of pursuit, uniting merely through necessity and dividing with the cessation of danger."[82] The failure of virtual representation to take effect in the New Jersey legislature, warned Governor William Livingston, was threatening the state with "anarchy and confusion."[83]

So far was the representative legislature becoming detached from the people that it was now not absurd to conceive of it as "an *extraneous power*."[84] Indeed, at the heart of constitutional developments in the decade following Independence was the opening of a gap between the people at large and their representatives in the state legislatures that had momentous implications for American political thought.

At the outset of the revolutionary movement the radical counties of Orange and Mecklenburg, North Carolina, as suspicious of the dominant Whig leaders as they were of the royal officials, expressed this distinction in a most explicit way. "Political power," they informed their delegates in the North Carolina convention of 1776, "is of two kinds, one principal and superior, the other derived and inferior.... The principal supreme power is possessed by the people at large, the derived and inferior power by the servants which they employ." With this crucial distinction between the people and all elected officials in hand, radical groups were able to make intelligible all sorts of restrictions on governmental, even legislative, authority, and to make comprehensible every important constitutional innovation of the revolutionary era. For "no authority can exist or be exercised but what shall appear to be ordained and created by the principal supreme power," and "whatever is constituted and ordained by the principal supreme power cannot be altered, suspended or abrogated by any other power."[85]

This vivid discrepancy between the people and all officials, representatives of the people included, was not anticipated by most Whigs in 1776, and even when it was, its significance was not readily appreciated. Yet the discrepancy was latent in the Whigs' fear of all political power and was always liable under the pressure of circumstances to be exposed.

Indeed, as early as 1775–76 during the drive for Independence many Whigs were pushed into arguments whose consequences they could scarcely have foreseen. The dissolution of the ordinary legislatures and the continued appeals to alternative bodies and to the nebulous will of the people in a state of nature rendered all institutions set above the people precarious and made representation itself suspect. Wherever revolutionary-minded Whigs found existing representative bodies, whether legislatures or conventions, reluctant to move with them, they entered a wedge between the people and those who supposedly spoke for them. They even urged that the people in the hesitant middle colonies rise up against their legal representatives, arguing that the people were so much in favor of "a total and final separation" from England that they would support Independence "even if the Conventions and Delegates of those Colonies vote against it."[86] It seemed obvious to some radicals in the Continental Congress "that the voice of the representatives is not always consonant with the voice of the people."[87] Although most Whigs in 1776 were not yet able or willing to draw out the implications of separating the people from their elected representatives in their new state governments, some did bring the whole idea of representation into question.

In various states in 1776 different groups—those most alienated from the existing centers of authority and least hopeful of controlling the legislatures of the newly constituted governments—expressed doubts over the ability of any representative body to speak conclusively for them. Both the freeholders of Albemarle County, Virginia, and the mechanics of New York City went so far as to deny the efficacy of representation altogether, arguing that the power of "approving, or disapproving, their own laws...ought forever to remain with the whole body of the people."[88] Not only in the ratifying of their constitution but even in the making of their laws, declared the New York Mechanics in a notable address of June 14, 1776, every man out of doors "is, or ought to be by inadmissible right, a co-legislator with all the other members of that community." Only the people at large were "the sole lawful legislature"; they could never really divest themselves completely of their "co-legislative power" to any set of representatives, "which, if repeatedly declared by us, to have been freely granted, would only proclaim our insanity, and for that reason, be void of themselves." The provincial congresses with their resolves or recommendations in place of laws seemed in fact more properly aware of their own limitations than previous legislatures had been and were thus to be commended for "so nobly asserting the rights which the people at large have to legislation. . . . Their laws, issued in the style of recommendations, leave inviolate, in the conventions, the committees, and finally the people at large, the right of rejection or ratification."[89]

The radicals in Pennsylvania actually carried this right of the people at large to legislate into constitutional form. Section 15 of the Pennsylvania constitution of 1776 provided that "all bills of public nature shall be printed for the consideration of the people, before they are read in general assembly the last time for debate and amendment: and except on occasions of sudden necessity, shall not be passed into laws until the next session of the assembly." Consequently, the representative assembly became a kind of upper house, while the people "out-of-doors" retained all their original power of legislation. This turned the elected representatives into an aristocracy of sorts, which was to be restrained by "the grand legislative Council, the People who had a right to approve or disapprove every bill" passed by the assembly.[90] "In a word," said one perceptive critic, "the new system of government for Pennsylvania destroys all ideas of representation."[91]

This disintegration of representation begun by the most suspicious and estranged groups in 1776 increasingly spread in the years after Independence, all the while being justified by an extension of republican Whig principles. "It has become absolutely necessary," wrote Benjamin Austin of Massachusetts, "that the 'majority of persons' should be cautioned against acquiescing in the sentiment of placing *implicit confidence* in their Representatives." Only "an *aristocratical party*," Austin charged, would want to inculcate such confidence in order that they might "persuade the *people*, that a *few men* know the things belonging to their political welfare much better than *themselves*."[92]

The people were increasingly urged to take back into their own hands the power they had delegated. The orthodox conviction that it was impossible to convene the people of a large state in the aggregate was, as one South Carolinian pamphleteer suggested, being proved wrong by the Americans. The people themselves in their riots and mobs, in their district committees and conventions, and in their explicit directions to their elected deputies seemed in fact to be replacing their representatives in the legislatures as the deliberative bodies for the states.[93] "Yes," declared an astonished Noah Webster, "*they legislate at home!*"[94]

Nearly every newspaper, pamphlet, and sermon of the 1780s dwelled on this breakdown of confidence between the people at large and their representative legislatures. The people, it appeared to those alarmed by these developments, were only pretending to give up their authority to their representatives, since they "afterwards reserve the right of making and of judging of all their laws themselves."[95] In Massachusetts in particular "the confidence of the people has been transferred from their Representatives in Court, to county Conventions, and from thence to a mob."[96] The Americans, it seemed, were being once again "LITERALLY placed on the broad field of nature."[97] Presumably the society had "never vested any body of men with any such power or authority, as bind the people to obedience or subjection." The acts of the several state legislatures had to be in the nature of tentative recommendations, since it was assumed "that as the people had all power originally in themselves; so they still retain it, to such a degree, that a majority of the people at large, have a right to reverse and annul every act and contract of all the legislatures on the continent."[98]

The people, complained a New Hampshire minister in 1784, were everywhere forming "combinations within the State in opposition to their own laws and government."[99] Actual representation was being extended to the point of weakening the binding character of law, leading, it seemed to many, "to anarchy and confusion" and tending "to dissolve and render nugatory every civil compact."[100]

It was not simply a problem of the breakdown of governmental authority. Not only were the people ignoring and disobeying the laws "merely because such measures do not coincide with their private views and separate interests," but the lawmakers in the legislatures were being bandied about and intimidated by electoral combinations and instructions in their local districts, pressured into thinking only of that "little circle with which they are immediately connected," out of a desire for "popular applause and their own advancement in office."[101] Self-appointed leaders of the people, "*demagogues*," "with the *vox populi vox Dei* in their mouths," men who were "at the bottom, *whether of yesterday or the day before,* who under plausible pretenses, . . . for dark, ambitious, or (not unlikely) speculative purposes, which they dare not own," were "disturbing the peace of the public, and causing the government to be bullied."[102] The legislatures, it was repeatedly claimed, were becoming simply the instruments and victims of parties and private combinations, puppets in the hands of narrow-minded, designing men. And no wonder, for "so long as the people shall be impressed with the idea, that they can, at any time, *constitutionally* control and direct the legislature, . . . they will be appealed to for that purpose, whenever men of popular talents shall be disappointed in their favourite schemes."[103]

It was at bottom a problem of representation, of the proper relationship between the people at large and their elected representatives, brought out most vehemently and fully in those states like Massachusetts and South Carolina where large numbers of people felt unable to satisfy their desires in the legislatures. It was in the seemingly most stable of the revolutionary states, however, in Maryland on the eve of the formation of the Federal Constitution, that the issue of representation underlying the politics of the decade was most pointedly and illuminatingly joined. The result was the longest and most significant constitutional debate of the Confederation period.

When the Maryland Senate turned down a series of paper money bills passed by the lower house in the late 1780s, the House of Delegates in a formal appeal in early 1787 urged the people at large to make their sense known on the money emissions "to both houses of the legislature." The lower house went on to argue that both houses of the legislature were bound by instructions of the people whenever they pleased to give them. "On a diversity in sentiment between us and the senate," the delegates told the people, "you alone are to decide, and to you only can there be any appeal." The senate replied cautiously, pointing out the serious consequences for the integrity of the legislature if instructions on such a question were allowed. "Once . . . appeal is made from the dictates of judgment to the voice of numbers," declared the senate, that "freedom of discussion and decision" which the constitution had explicitly intended for the upper house would be taken away.[104]

Mild as the senate's reply was, polemicists jumped on it as insidiously and subtly asserting that the senate was "independent *of the people*, and not bound by their instructions in any case." The whole issue seemed dangerously close to getting out of hand. Petitions to be presented to the legislature had been circulating throughout all the counties, calling for a clear understanding once and for all of the position of the senate in the government. "Since the Revolution, and the Establishment of our present Form of Government," declared the petition, "it cannot be questioned, that both Branches of our Legislature are the Representatives and Trustees of the People," and that from the political relation between representative and constituent, the representative must always speak and execute the sense of the constituent whenever it was collected and communicated to him. It made no difference, wrote Samuel Chase, that the senate was elected indirectly. "Both branches of our legislature derive all their power from the people, and *equally* hold their *commissions* to legislate, or make laws, from the *grant* of the people; and there is no difference between them but *only* in the *duration of their commission.* Their authority proceeds from the same source, and is co-equal, and co-extensive. . . . The people are equally the *constituents of both.*" The legislature was divided into "two distinct bodies of men" only that they might "operate as *checks* upon each other."[105]

These were new thoughts for Maryland, and they bore no resemblance, as one writer pointed out, to the assumptions of the framers of the constitution, Samuel Chase included, who in 1776 had intended the senate to represent "the aristocratical part of the government."[106] With the spread of egalitarian sentiments, however, no one dared defend the senate on those grounds now. If the senators, said Thomas Stone, the drafter of the senate's reply to the house of delegates, ever "set themselves in opposition to the great body of the people of this State," they would undoubtedly be "objects to be confined for insanity than dreaded as tyrants." The supporters of the senate thus understandably avoided any probing discussion of the distinctive character of the upper house. They conceded that the senate was as representative of the people as the lower house and instead concentrated on the problem of instructions, denying that either branch of the legislature could be commanded by the people.[107]

The defenders of the senate began their opposition to instructions with a conventional defense of the notion of virtual representation. The people, they readily admitted, were the source of all political power; but the people could express this power only through periodic elections, not through binding instructions to their representatives. "The supreme power of legislation is in the people—but when they choose representatives to make laws, they are bound by the laws that shall be so made." All the people's original powers "are invested in the legislature, and are not reserved in the people." Representation was not "limited, confined, or imperfect." Instead the representative had a full and general power to transact business for his constituent: "whatever he may do, will be binding on the principal; notwithstanding the business was not done agreeable to his opinion and sentiments; and he has no remedy, but to appoint another representative to do his business in future."[108]

Judge Alexander Hanson, emerging as the principal opponent of legislative instructions, repeated this same line of argument throughout the spring and summer of 1787— a line of argument that might have made sense in Edmund Burke's England but was increasingly out of touch with

American realities. "All power indeed flows from the people," conceded Hanson, "but the doctrine that the power, actually, at all times, resides in the people, is subversive of all government and law." As John Locke and other Whigs had shown, representative government meant that "the legislative possesses the only power of making laws," a power that lasted until the next election or the dissolution of the government. Instructions to delegates from a particular county on some special parochial concern, Hanson admitted, may be allowable, but surely not in this case where "national" instructions from all counties simultaneously were to be directed at both branches of the legislature. This in effect, said Hanson, gave the people at large a lawmaking capacity outside the legislature, making them literally "masters" of their "servants" in the legislature, an idea that was "one of the most incongruous and absurd, that ever entered into a human brain." The representatives, once elected, must be independent legislators, free to deliberate on the public good; they thus could not be "mere tools" of the people. Yet those who believed in binding instructions must "erroneously imagine the constitutional legislature to be nothing more than agents, deputies, or trustees."[109]

Erroneous or not, this was precisely what many Americans believed their representatives to be—mere agents or tools of the people, who could give binding directions "whenever they please to give them." The people's power, declared Samuel Chase, in an image borrowed from the British radical James Burgh, "is like the light of the sun, native, original, inherent, and unlimited by human authority. Power in the rulers or governors of the people is like the reflected light of the moon, and is only borrowed, delegated and limited by the grant of the people." Every elected official was equally a representative of the people. "From the nature of a government by *representation,* the *deputies* must be subject to the will of their *principals* or this manifest absurdity and plain consequence must follow, that a *few* men would be *greater* than the *whole* community, and might act in *opposition* to the *declared* sense of *all their constituents.*"[110]

"The legislature are the trustees of the people and accountable to them," asserted William Paca, who assumed the principal burden of defending the instructions. All the great Whigs—Locke, Molesworth, Trenchard, Hampden, and Sidney—had upheld this trusteeship relation between constituents and representatives. Therefore, the "people only" could be "the *constitutional judges* of *legislative* or *public* oppressions," best exercised through their right of instructing. The "question" being debated here in Maryland, said Paca, was "not upon the *right* or *force* of instruction from a particular county, city, or borough, but upon the *right* and *force* of the *national voice* communicated and declared to the legislature by memorial, remonstrance, or INSTRUCTION, from *every* county, city, and borough, or the majority of the nation." Thus, Paca concluded, the people at large through this broadened use of positive instructions on general questions of public interest were in fact capable of doing what no eighteenth-century thinker considered possible for so large a society: participating in the exercise of legislative authority "*personally*" as well as "*representationally.*"[111]

It soon became evident that the debate was carrying well beyond the question of instructions and threatening to shatter the categories of government that had dominated Western thinking for centuries. By arguing that the Maryland Senate was as representative a body as the house of representatives and was therefore capable of being instructed by the people at large, the Maryland radicals were actually calling into question the traditional theory of mixed government. The right of the people to instruct their representatives was an old tradition in Maryland, said Samuel Chase; and Marylanders had frequently exercised this right of instructing their delegates in the former proprietary government, and had in fact instructed Chase himself in the convention of 1776. Of course, admitted Chase, the people had never previously claimed any right to instruct the members of the upper house, since they had been appointed by the proprietor and thus in fact had been his representatives and not the people's. But now under the new republican government the situation was different: "By our constitution," Chase told the people, "*you* do appoint the Senate, and they are, and have *uniformly* claimed themselves to be, your *representatives.*" And as "your representatives, they are bound by your instructions, or you destroy the very idea of *election* and of *delegating* power"—but only if election and the delegation of power by the people had become, as they had for Chase and for other Americans in these years, the sole criterion of representation.[112]

If logically carried out, this electoral basis of representation would turn every elected official into a kind of representative of the people. Those opposed to the instructing of the Maryland Senate saw the implications and tried to resist them. Suppose, suggested Alexander Hanson, that the people of Maryland had instituted a different form of government in 1776. "It was debated in convention," he said, "whether there should not be three distinct branches of the legislature. Had the proposition been adopted, would you have called them all agents, deputies, or trustees, subject to the order of their principal?" Would the governor simply by being elected by the people become their representative capable of being instructed by them? Yet once it was admitted that the senate, because elective, was as equally representative of the people as the lower house, it was difficult to deny this sort of pervasion of representation in a republic. "If the people who have a common right of suffrage claim a right to instruct the Senate, as ultimately chosen by them," cried one Marylander, "by a parity in reasoning, the Governor and Council, Delegates to Congress, and Judges of our Courts are liable to be instructed by them."[113]

Hanson in particular wrestled with the troublesome implications of his concession that the senate was representative of the people and fumbled with the new and peculiar problems of politics being created in America. It was quite explicable, he said, that "writing on so important a subject" he had had "no recourse to authority" or quotations to buttress his arguments. For nowhere could he find a writer before himself who had examined "the case of a legislature, consisting of two distinct bodies of men, deriving their authority immediately or ultimately, from the act of the people." The classical categories of government were of little help in untangling the knotted lines of American political thinking, since America no longer seemed governed by the one, the few, or the many, or even by all together. "When the legitimate power is in the people at large," wrote Hanson in an attempt at a clarification useful for his purposes, "it is truly the government of the people, or a strict democracy." However, "when society enters into a solemn compact, prescribing modes of election by the people, whereby a select body or two, or more select bodies, shall be for ever kept up, to legislate for the people, this is another form of government. This is the government by representation." The proponents of national instructions, by urging the people at large to "deliberate for themselves, and prescribe laws," had turned Maryland's constitution into a "government of the people, confounded with the government of representation, or properly no regular government at all."[114]

Government by representation was thus all-pervasive and excluded the presence of democracy from the constitution entirely. Squeezed between his admission of the representative character of the senate and his desire to maintain the independence of the legislature from continual popular dictation, Hanson, like others in the same years for different reasons, found himself inventing a new category of politics. The American states were neither simple democracies nor traditional mixed governments. They had become in all branches governments by representation.

The use of binding instructions and the growing sense that the representative was merely a limited agent or spokesman for the local interests of his constituents in the decade after Independence ate away the independent authority of the representative and distorted, even destroyed, the traditional character of representation. Evidently the people could never be fully embodied in their houses of representatives; sovereignty and the ultimate power to make law, as the extralegislative devices developing in this period illustrated, remained with the collective people. The logic of these developments was to take the people out of the government altogether and to blur the previous distinction among representatives, senators, and magistrates.

Once the supposed representatives of the people (the

democratic element) in the lower houses of the legislature were regarded with the same suspicion and uneasiness as the traditional rulers and upper houses (the monarchical and aristocratic elements) had been (representation was after all, said one Virginian, "at best, but a species of aristocracy"), it became a much simpler matter to view the rulers and senators in the same light as the supposed representatives were viewed.[115] Once the American atmosphere of suspicion and jealousy eroded the mutuality of interests between representatives and people that made representation what it was to most eighteenth-century Englishmen, the only criterion of representation left was election, which helps explain the Americans' increasing focus on the right to vote as a measure of representation.

With election or simply the derivation of authority from the people becoming the sole basis and measure of representation, the several branches of the government began to seem indistinguishable—all somehow representative of the people. Advocates for an upper house in Pennsylvania, whose radical constitution of 1776 provided for only a unicameral legislature, discovered that they could no longer justify a senate in the traditional terms of mixed government: any talk of embodying an aristocracy in the government smacked of a House of Lords and was immediately jumped upon. Thus those who wanted a senate for Pennsylvania were compelled to justify it as simply "a double representation of the people," made necessary by the need to divide a mistrusted political power.[116] But if the people could be represented by two institutions at the same time, why couldn't they be represented by three or four or more institutions? Suddenly, the people could be everywhere in government, and the theory of mixed government had lost its meaning.

All elected officials could now be considered as kinds of representatives of the people, as equally trusted or mistrusted agents of the people. "In our republican government," the people could now be told, "not only our *Deputies,* but our *Governor* and *Council* may in a good sense be esteemed our representatives, as they are annually chosen by you, to manage our public affairs."[117] After all, "who have we in America but the people? Members of congress, of assemblies, or councils, are still a part of the people. Their honours do not take them out of the aggregate body."[118]

It was not unreasonable now to argue that "the principle for Representation" should be extended "throughout every public body" so that all elected, hence representative, officials—senators or others—should be elected in proportion to the population, the logic of which was finally realized by the Supreme Court in its state reapportionment decisions of the 1960s nearly two centuries later.[119] "In a free State," wrote Thomas Tudor Tucker of South Carolina in 1784, "every officer, from the Governor to the constable, is, so far as the powers of his office extend, as truly the representative of the people, as a member of the legislature; and his act, within the appointed limitation, is the act of the people: for he is their agent, and derives his authority from them."[120]

The people no longer actually shared in a part of the government (as, for example, the people of England participated in their government through the House of Commons), but they remained outside the entire government, watching, controlling, pulling the strings for all their agents in every branch or part of the government. They embraced the whole government, and no branch or part could speak with the complete authority of the people. Indeed, not even all parts of the government collectively incorporated the full powers of the people. "With us it would be an absurd surrender of liberty to delegate full powers to any set of men whatever." Conventions, assemblies, senates, magistracy, were all agents of the people for certain limited purposes. Only such a conception of representation made sense of the remarkable constitutional developments of the Confederation period—the use of instructions, the electioneering, and the extralegislative organizations, in particular the special constituting conventions creating a superior law ratifiable by the people themselves in their sovereign capacity and hence unalterable by the people's provisional agents in the legislatures. "Delegates," said Tucker, "may be sent to a convention with powers, under certain restrictions, to frame a constitution. Delegates are sent to the General Assembly with powers, under certain restrictions prescribed . . . by a previously established compact or constitution, to make salutary laws." Yet, concluded Tucker, neither the convention nor the assembly possessed the total authority of the people. "If either one or the other should exceed the powers vested in them, their act is no longer the act of their constituents." The power of the people outside the government was always absolute and untrammeled; that of their various delegates in the government could never be.[121]

These were revolutionary ideas that had unfolded rapidly in the decade after Independence, but not deliberately or evenly. Men were always only half aware of where their thought was going, for these new ideas about politics were not the products of extended, reasoned analysis but were rather numerous responses of various Americans to a swiftly changing reality, of men involved in endless polemics compelled to contort and draw out from the prevailing assumptions the latent logic few had foreseen. Rarely before 1787 were these new thoughts comprehended by anyone as a whole. They were bits and pieces thrown up by the necessities of argument and condition, without broad design or significance. But if crystallized by sufficient pressure they could result in a mosaic of an entirely new conception of politics to those who would attempt to describe it. The creation of a new federal government in 1787 provided that kind of pressure.

The Federalists and the Anti-Federalists on Representative Government

REPRESENTATION WAS JUST AS MUCH THE CENTRAL issue underlying the debates over the Federal Constitution in 1787–88 as it had been during the debates over the nature of the British Empire two decades earlier. In fact the debate over the Constitution raised once again the old distinction between actual and virtual representation. At the very time the social assumptions that made virtual representation comprehensible were disintegrating, the Federalists, as the supporters of the Constitution called themselves, found the need for some sort of virtual representation more imperative than ever before. Through the structural devices of the new federal government they sought to perpetuate an elitist conception of representation even though political and social conditions in America were making a continuation of such elite rule difficult if not impossible to sustain.

The opponents of the Constitution, the Anti-Federalists, as they were called, offered a spirited defense of the most localist and particularist kind of representation voiced in the entire revolutionary era, an actuality of representation that was much more in accord with America's social and political realities than the sort of representation advocated by the Federalists. Yet the representational issue between the supporters and the opponents of the Constitution was never this clear, for the Federalists did not justify their form of virtual representation in traditional terms. They did not attempt to confront head-on the developments in the idea of actual representation that had taken place during the previous decade; instead, they effectively used and exploited the emerging implications of actual representation for very contrary purposes. In the end they defeated the Anti-Federalists and their defense of localism by turning actual representation against itself.

The Federalists saw the problems of American politics in the 1780s as stemming from its intense localism. Not only had "the great objects of the nation" been "sacrificed constantly to local views," declared Gouverneur Morris in the Constitutional Convention, but "the general interests of the States had been sacrificed to those of the Counties," lost in the scramble for private advantages and local favors.[122] Such developments had occurred precisely because "the best people," people like the Federalist leaders themselves, had lost control of politics. "Instead of choosing men for their abilities, integrity and patriotism," the people in the various local constituencies had chosen men because they would "vote for a new town, or a new county, or in favour of a memorial," constantly mistaking "the particular circle" in which they moved for "the general voice" of the society.[123] They had elected to their state legislatures men such as William Findley of Pennsylvania, a former weaver, and Abraham Yates of New York, a former cobbler, men who lacked the cosmopolitan outlook of college-educated gentlemen. The "spirit of locality" that such narrow-minded and illiberal men promoted, concluded James Madison in 1788, was "inseparable" from the American practice of electing representatives from small districts or towns.[124]

Hence the Federalist remedy for the vices of American politics, embodied in the new national government, focused on radically changing the scale and the process of representation. The House of Representatives in the new national government would contain only sixty-five members and would thus be smaller than most of the state legislatures. When these sixty-five were compared with the thousand or more representatives in the state legislatures, the Federalists' desire to transcend the states and narrow the representation at the national level became clear. If the people of a particular state—North Carolina, for example—had to elect only five men to the federal Congress in contrast to the two hundred and thirty-two they elected to their state assembly, they would be far more likely to ignore the illiberal, parochial men with "factious tempers" and "local prejudices" who were dominating the state legislatures in the 1780s, and instead elect to the new federal government only those college-educated few who were, in James Wilson's words, "men of intelligence and uprightness."[125] These few gentry, it was hoped, would virtually represent all the diverse interests and occupations of the whole of American society.

By greatly enlarging the electoral districts and by severely decreasing the number of those who would represent the people and wield effective political power, the Federalists expected to free America from the evils of localism that had become so glaringly evident during the previous decade. The great height of the new government, its great distance from parochial interests, would hopefully prevent the obscure and narrow-minded men who had gained power in the state governments from scaling its walls. The new federal government, said Madison, would act as a kind of sieve filtering "from the mass of the society the purest and noblest characters which it contains."[126] Those who would represent the people in the federal legislature, because of their fewness of numbers and the breadth of their electorate, would be "the best men in the country," those natural social leaders "who possess," in Madison's words, "the most attractive merit and the most diffusive and established characters."[127] "For," wrote John Jay in *Federalist* No. 3, "although town or county, or other contracted influence, may place men in State assemblies, or senates, or courts of justice, or executive departments, yet more general and extensive reputation for talents and other qualifications will be necessary to recommend men to offices under the national government."[128]

The political and social implications of the Federalists' proposal were not lost on the Anti-Federalists, and they countered the Federalists' artificially contrived device for establishing virtual representation with a vehement defense of actual representation. Society, even in the separate states, they reminded the Federalists over and over, was not a unitary, organic hierarchy for which an elite of gentlemen could sympathetically speak, but was rather a heterogeneous mixture of "many different classes or orders of people, Merchants, Farmers, Planter Mechanics and Gentry or wealthy Men," each possessing distinct and often incompatible interests. In such a society men from one class or group, however educated or respectable, could never be acquainted with the "Situation and Wants" of those of another class or group.[129]

Representation, said the Anti-Federalists, had to be truly replication; each local constituency, occupation, or interest had to represent itself directly. "Farmers, traders and mechanics...all ought to have a competent number of their best informed members in the legislature."[130] It was not enough that the representatives were for the people, declared the Anti-Federalists in the starkest articulation of actual representation made in the revolutionary era; if the representatives were to know intimately the people's "feelings, circumstances, and interest," they had to be truly of them. Only ordinary men, men not distinguished by the characteristics of aristocratic wealth, education, and taste, could be trusted to speak for what were increasingly referred to as "the middling and lower classes of people."[131]

The Anti-Federalists thus came to oppose the new national government for the very reason the Federalists favored it: because its very structure and detachment from the people would work to exclude any kind of actual and local-interest representation and prevent ordinary middling men from exercising political power. It went almost without saying that the awesome president and the exalted Senate would be dangerously far removed from the people. But even the "democratic branch" of the government, the House of Representatives, which presumably should "possess the same interests and opinions that the people themselves would possess, were they all assembled," was, with its scant sixty-five members, only "a mere shred or rag" of the people's power, and hardly a match for the monarchical and aristocratic branches of the government.[132] When the number of representatives was "so small," declared the Anti-Federalists of Pennsylvania, "the office will be highly elevated and distinguished; the style in which the members live will probably be high; circumstances of this kind will render the place of a representative not a desirable one to sensible, substantial men, who have been used to walk in the plain and frugal paths of life."[133] While the ordinary people in extensive electoral districts with thirty or forty thousand inhabitants would remain "divided," those with "conspicuous military, popular, civil or legal talents" could more easily form broader associations to dominate elections; they had family and other connections to "unite their interests."[134]

If only a half-dozen congressmen were to be selected to represent a large state, rarely then, argued the Anti-Federalists in terms that were essentially no different from those implied by the Federalists in the Constitution's defense, would persons from "the great body of the people, the middle and lower classes," be elected to the House of Representatives.[135] "The Station is too high and exalted to be filled but [by] the *first Men* in the State in point of Fortune and Influence. In fact no order or class of the people will be represented in the House of Representatives called the Democratic Branch but the rich and wealthy."[136] All that Americans had learned from the Revolution about the need to maintain the closest possible connections between constituents and representatives seemed to the Anti-Federalists to be threatened by the new Federal Constitution.[137]

The Federalists realized only too keenly what the nature of the popular attack on the Constitution would be when it went forth from the Philadelphia Convention. "Aristocracy," warned John Dickinson in the Convention, "will be the watchword; the Shibboleth among its adversaries."[138] Precisely because the Anti-Federalists, as Alexander Hamilton observed in the New York ratifying convention, did talk "so often of an aristocracy," the Federalists were compelled in the ratification debates to minimize and obscure the elitist nature of the representational system they were creating.[139] An open defense of the orthodox doctrine of virtual representation, with all that it implied of an organic and hierarchical conception of society ruled by a natural elite, smacked too much of aristocracy.

To be sure, Hamilton himself attempted in *Federalist* No. 35 to challenge directly the Anti-Federalist advocacy of an explicit class or local-interest representation by recalling the traditional organic unity of society that tied ordinary people and the elite together. "The idea of an actual representation of all classes of the people, by persons of each class," he wrote, "is altogether visionary." Electing artisans and tradesmen to the legislatures was impractical and unnecessary. "Mechanics and manufacturers will always be inclined, with few exceptions, to give their votes to merchants, in preference to persons of their own professions or trades.... They know that the merchant is their natural patron and friend; and they are aware, that however great the confidence they may justly feel in their own good sense, their interests can be more effectually promoted by the merchant than by themselves." Not only were the artisans and tradesmen caught up in their occupations, but they lacked "those acquired endowments, without which, in a deliberated assembly, the greatest natural abilities are the most part useless." The same was true with the landed interest. "The opulent landholder and the middling farmer" tended to have "a common interest." But even if they didn't, there was no reason to fear that men of "moderate property, or of no property at all," would not be elected to the Congress, especially since people were free to choose whomever they had the most confidence in.

As far as "the learned professions" were concerned, and here Hamilton meant essentially lawyers like himself, they were the ideal representatives. "They truly form no distinct interest in society, and according to their situation and talents, will be indiscriminately the objects of the confidence and choice of each other, and of other parts of the community." They will know how to legislate. They "will feel a neutrality to the rivalships between the different branches of industry," and were most "likely to prove an impartial arbiter between them," and most capable of promoting in a disinterested manner whatever interest will be "conducive to the general interest of the society." Wasn't it better, asked Hamilton, to have as a representative a "man whose situation leads to extensive inquiry and information" than someone "whose observation does not travel beyond the circle of his neighbors and acquaintances?" Such a farsighted, cosmopolitan representative would know the "dispositions and inclinations" of his fellow citizens and would be capable of creating "strong chords of sympathy" between himself and his constituents.

Yet such a traditional paternalistic conception of society, together with its concomitant idea of virtual representation, seemed increasingly outmoded for America. Instead of trying to defend the conception of an organic hierarchical society and virtual representation, Madison and many other Federalists realized that they would be better off rooting their promotion of the new Constitution in the realities of American political practices, in the developing implications of actual and local representation itself. If the Federalists were to convince Americans that the new Constitution was "strictly republican," then they would have to find an explanation of the new government that took account of what was happening to the process of representation in America.

It was out of the developments of the Revolution, particularly those developments related to the practices and implications of actual representation, that the Federalists fashioned their most powerful defense of the new federal system. Confronted with the Anti-Federalists' fears of a far-removed and aristocratic national power, the Federalists were compelled to emphasize and exaggerate the popular and representative character of the new federal government.

"The federal representatives will represent *the people*," the Federalists said, "they will be *the people;* and it is not *probable* they will abuse themselves." They will be "ourselves; the men of our own choice, in whom we can confide; whose interest is inseparably connected with our own. Why is it, then, that gentlemen speak of Congress as some foreign body, as a set of men who will seek every opportunity to enslave us?" The opponents of the Constitution, said the Federalists, threaten us "with the loss of our liberties by the possible abuse of power, notwithstanding the maxim, that those who give may take away. It is the people that give power, and can take it back. What shall restrain them? They are the masters who give it, and of whom their servants hold it." Thus there could be no real difference between the Congress and the state legislatures. "Are they not both the servants of the people? Are not Congress and the state legislatures the agents of the people, and are they not to consult the good of the people?" "Congress can have no other power than the states had." "To whom do we delegate these powers?" the Federalists asked over and over. "To our own representatives," they answered. "Why should we fear so much greater dangers from our representatives there, than from those we have here? Why make so great a distinction between our representatives here, and in the federal government, where every branch is formed on the same principle—preserving throughout the representative, responsible character?"[140]

Such radical Federalist arguments—suggesting that both the state and federal governments and, indeed, all branches of all the governments were equally representative of the people—were made possible and comprehensible by what had happened to the nature of representation and political power during the previous two decades. By contending that all elected officials, at both the state and federal levels, were equal agents of the people, the Federalists unleashed ideas about representation that had all sorts of unanticipated consequences. If the people could be simultaneously represented twice, then presumably there could be no end to the number of representatives or agents created by the people.

Indeed, since all governmental power in a republic, whatever its nature or function, was something of a delegation by the people, all parts of a republican system now seemed representative, essentially indistinguishable in their character. It was surprising, said John Dickinson, that some critics had declared that the Constitution was not sufficiently representative of the people, even "though the *whole people* of the United States are to be *trebly* represented in it in *three different modes* of representation."[141] Since, as

Tench Coxe said, every office either will be "the immediate gift" of the people or "will come from them through
the hands of their servants," every officer was to be equally
representative of the people.[142] Not only was the Senate as
representative of the people as the lower house, but even, as
Hamilton declared in the New York ratifying convention,
"the President of the United States will be himself the representative of the people."[143] Since the Federalists were eager to justify both the new national government and stron-
ger senates and executives everywhere, they were inevitably
driven to argue that all governmental officials at all levels
were more or less equal representatives of the people.

Although the members of the houses of representatives
were perhaps the more "immediate representatives," no
longer were they the full and exclusive representatives of
the people. "The Senators," said Nathaniel Chipman, "are
to be representatives of the people, no less, in fact, than the
members of the other house."[144] Foreigners, noted William Vans Murray, had mistaken the upper houses in the
legislatures in America as some sort of an embodiment of
an aristocracy. Even in Maryland and in the Federal Constitution where the senates were indirectly elected, the
upper house was derived mediately from the people. "It
represents the people," said Murray. "It represents no particular order of men or of ranks."[145] To those who sought
to comprehend fully the integrity of the new system the
senate could only be a weight in the powers of legislative
deliberation, not a weight of property, of privileges, or of
interests. Election by the people, not the number of cham-
bers in the legislature, declared John Stevens of New Jersey,
had made "our governments the most democratic that ever

existed anywhere."[146] "With us," concluded James Wilson, "the power of magistrates, call them by whatever name you please, are the grants of the people."[147]

Therefore, said the Federalists, all governmental officials, including even the executive and judicial parts of the government, were agents of the people, not fundamentally different from the people's nominal representatives in the lower houses of the legislatures. The Americans of 1776, observed Wilson, had not clearly understood the nature of their executives and judiciaries. Although the authority of their governors and judges became in 1776 as much "the child of the people" as that of the legislatures, the people could not forget their traditional colonial aversion to the executive and judiciary and their fondness for their legislatures, which under the British monarchy had been the guardians of their rights and the anchor of their political hopes. "Even at this time," Wilson noted with annoyance, "people can scarcely divest themselves of those opposite prepossessions." The legislatures often were still called "the *people's representatives*," implying, "though probably, not avowed upon reflection," that the executive and judicial powers were not so strongly or closely connected with the people. "But it is high time," said Wilson, "that we should chastise our prejudices." The different parts of the government were functionally but not substantively or socially different. "The executive and judicial powers are now drawn from the same source, are now animated by the same principles, and are now directed to the same ends, with the legislative authority: they who execute, and they who administer the laws, are so much the servants, and therefore as much the friends of the people, as those who make them."[148] The entire government, including even judges, had become the limited agency of the sovereign people who were not fully embodied anywhere.

Viewing all parts of the government, even judges, as disembodied agents of the people had curious consequences; none of these agents or even all of them together seemed to speak completely and authoritatively for the people, who continued to exist even after all their servants were elected or appointed. Some now saw the supposed lawmaking of the legislatures as simply the promulgating of decrees to which the people, standing outside the entire government, had never given their full and unqualified assent. It was even possible to contend, as one Rhode Islander did in 1787, that all acts of a legislature were in effect temporary edicts, which were still "liable to examination and scrutiny by the people, that is, by the Supreme Judiciary, their servants for this purpose; and those that militate with the fundamental laws, or impugn the principles of the constitution, are to be judicially set aside as void, and of no effect."[149]

It was Alexander Hamilton who most fully drew out the implications of viewing the judiciary as another kind of representative of the people. The so-called representatives of the people in the state legislatures, wrote Hamilton in *Federalist* No. 78, did not really embody the people, as Parliament, for example, presumably embodied the people of Britain. On the contrary, the state legislators were really only one kind of servant of the people with a limited delegated authority to act on their behalf. Americans, said Hamilton, had no intention of allowing "the representatives of the people to substitute their *will* to that of their constituents." In fact, it was "far more rational to suppose, that the courts were designed to be an intermediate body between the people and the legislature, in order, among other things, to keep the latter within the limits assigned their authority."

Conceiving of judges as just another kind of servant of the sovereign people helped to made possible the emerging practice of what came to be called judicial review. The authority of the judges to set aside acts of the legislatures, said Hamilton, lay in the fact that in America real and ultimate sovereignty rested with the people themselves, not with their representative agents in the legislatures. Judicial review, said Hamilton, did not "by any means suppose a superiority of the judicial to the legislative power. It only supposes that the power of the people is superior to both; and that where the will of the legislature declared in its statutes, stands in opposition to that of the people, declared in the constitution, the judges...ought to regulate their decisions by the fundamental laws, rather than by those which are not fundamental."[150]

Other Americans grasped the implications of judges being just another kind of agent or servant of the people and concluded that they therefore should be elected, as the other agents of the people were. Although this logic would not be followed out in practice until the middle decades of the nineteenth century, the Jeffersonian Democratic-Republican radical John Leland made this point very explicitly in 1805. "The election of all officers, to fill all parts of the government," he said, "is the natural genius that presides over the United States....If men are incompetent to elect their judges, they are equally incompetent to appoint others to do it for them." Judges should not be immune to the authority of the people. "A judicial monarch is a character as abhorrent as an executive or legislative monarch."[151]

In the succeeding decades of the nineteenth century, many of the states, especially the new states of the West, began electing their judges. And today at least thirty-nine states elect their judges, which presumably helps to guarantee their independence from the other parts of the government.

Although the Federalists had scarcely ever desired an elected judiciary, they had set that development in motion with their argument that judges were agents of the people not all that different from the people's agents in the legislatures. Their argument in 1780s, however, did have the immediate effect of rescuing the judiciary from its earlier eighteenth-century insignificance and identification with the executive magistracy and transforming it into an equal and independent partner in a modern tripartite government of legislative, executive, and judicial branches.

With these new conceptions of popular representation firmly in the Federalist grasp, all the Anti-Federalists' "rage for democracy, and zeal for the rights of the people" could be turned back upon them, and the Federalists could argue "with truth" that the supporters of the Constitution were "true republicans, and by no means less attached to liberty than those who oppose it."[152] The ultimate consequence of the Federalists' arguments was a totally new conception of politics.

The End of Classical Politics

EVEN BEFORE THE DEBATE OVER THE CONSTITUTION was settled, many Americans began recognizing the peculiar significance of their political achievement. Apparently they had not entirely understood politics at the outset of the Revolution, but within a decade they believed they had come to comprehend the true principles of republicanism and to incorporate them in their various state governments. But it was the new Federal Constitution that most fully expressed all they had learned. "The government of the United States," wrote Nathaniel Chipman of Vermont in 1793, "exhibits a new scene in the political history of the world, exhibits, in theory, the most beautiful system, which has yet been devised by the wisdom of man."[153] With their governments the Americans had placed the science of politics on a footing with the other great scientific discoveries of the previous century. Their governments, said William Vans Murray, represented "the most finished political forms" in history and had "deservedly attracted the attention of all speculative minds."[154] Their creation of a new political theory was in fact the essence of their Revolution. "The independence of America considered merely as a separation from England, would have been a matter but of little importance," remarked Thomas Paine, "had it not been accompanied by a revolution in the principles and practise of governments."[155]

Their governments were so new and so distinctive that they groped for political terms adequate to describe them. By the late 1780s many Americans were calling their governments democracies, but peculiar kinds of democracies. America, said Murray, had established governments that were "in their principles, structure, and whole mass, purely and unalterably Democratic."[156] The American republics, remarked John Stevens, approached "nearer to perfect democracies" than any other governments in the world.[157] Yet democracy, as eighteenth-century political scientists generally understood the term, was not, they realized, a wholly accurate description of their new governments. They were "Democratic Republics," as Nathaniel Chipman called them, by which was "meant, a Representative Democracy."[158]

In *Federalist* No. 10 Madison called the American governments republics, as distinct from a "pure democracy" in which a small number of citizens assembled and administered the government in person. For Madison a republic had become a species of government to be classed alongside aristocracy or democracy, a distinctive form of government "in which the scheme of representation takes place."[159]

Representation—that was the key conception in unlocking an understanding of the American political system. America was, as Hamilton said, "a *representative democracy*."[160] Only the American governmental scheme, wrote Thomas Paine, was based "wholly on the system of representation," and thus the United States was "the only real republic in character and practise, that now exists."The American polity, said Paine, was "representation ingrafted upon democracy," creating "a system of government capable of embracing and confederating all the various interests and every extent of territory and population."[161]

It was representation then—"the delegation of the government" said Madison, "to a small number of citizens elected by the rest"—that explained the uniqueness of the American polities.[162] "The *principle* on which all the American governments are founded," wrote Samuel Williams of Vermont, "is *representation*."[163] No other nation, said Charles Pinckney of South Carolina, so enjoyed the right of self-government, "where the true principles of representation are understood and practised, and where all authority flows from and returns at stated periods to, the people." Representation, said Edmund Randolph, was "a thing not understood in its full extent till very lately."[164] Neither the Israelites nor the ancients had properly comprehended the uses of representation—"a very excellent modern improvement in the management of republics," said Samuel Langdon of New Hampshire.[165]

James Wilson of Pennsylvania, perhaps the most underrated of the founders, offered the most elaborate explanation of America's distinctive system of representation. "It is surprising, indeed," he said, "how very imperfectly, at this day, the doctrine of representation is understood in Europe. Even Great Britain," he pointed out, "which boasts a superior knowledge of the subject, and is generally supposed to have carried it into practice, falls far short of its true and genuine principles." Representation, said Wilson, barely touched the English constitution, since it was not immediately or remotely the source of executive or judicial power. Even in the Parliament representation was not "a pervading principle," but actually was only a check, confined to the House of Commons. The Lords acted either under hereditary right or under an authority granted by the prerogative of the Crown and hence were "not the representatives of the people." The world, it seemed, had "left to America the glory and happiness of forming a government where representation shall at once supply the basis and the cement of the superstructure."[166]

"In America," said Samuel Williams, "every thing tended to introduce, and to complete the system of representation."[167] America, wrote Madison, had created the first example of "a government wholly popular, and founded at the same time, wholly on that principle [of representation]."[168] Americans had made their entire system from top to bottom representative, "diffusing," in Wilson's words, "this vital principle throughout all the different divisions and departments of the government." Since Americans, influenced by the implications of the developing conception of actual representation, now clearly believed that "the right of representing is conferred by the act of electing," every part of the elective governments had become representative of the people.[169] In truth, said Madison, representation was "the pivot" on which the whole American system moved.[170]

The people at large, said the Federalists in a ready concession to the realities of actual representation, could never be totally eclipsed by the process of representation, as, for example, the people of England were eclipsed by their representation in the House of Commons. In England, once the House of Commons was elected, the people went out of existence until the next election. But this was not true in America. Even after electing their agents, the American people never lost their political presence.

Ultimately, these contrasting ideas of representation separated the English and American constitutional systems. In England Parliament came to possess sovereignty—the final, supreme, and indivisible lawmaking authority in the state—because it embodied the whole society, all the estates of the realm, within itself, and nothing existed outside it. In America, however, sovereignty remained with the people themselves—and not with any of their agents or even with all their agents put together. The American people, unlike the English, were never eclipsed by the process of representation.

When Americans referred to the sovereignty of the people, they did not just mean that all government was derived from the people. Instead, they meant that the final, supreme, and indivisible lawmaking authority of the society remained with the people themselves, not with their representatives or with any of their agents.

In America the notion that sovereignty rested in the people was therefore not just a convenient political fiction; the American people, unlike the English, retained an actual lawmaking authority. Only by conceiving of sovereignty remaining with the people could Americans make sense of the doctrine of federalism, where, contrary to the prevailing thought of the eighteenth century, both the state and federal legislatures were to be equally representative of the people at the same time, "both," said Edmund Pendleton of Virginia, "possessed of our equal confidence—both chosen in the same manner, and equally responsible to us."[171] "The federal and state governments," wrote Madison in

Federalist No. 46, "are in fact but different agents and trustees of the people, constituted with different powers, and designed for different purposes."

This conception of sovereignty remaining with the people at large made sense too of America's new constitutional achievements, such as the special constitution-making conventions and the process of popular ratification of constitutions. Eventually, it also made possible the emergence of peculiar institutions and processes of the early twentieth century and indeed of our own time. The primaries, referendums, processes of recall, and ballot initiatives introduced by Progressive reformers at the beginning of the twentieth century and used with great effectiveness in our own time were only extensions of the ideas of popular sovereignty and acute actual representation created during these debates over the ratification of the Constitution.

The pervasive Whig mistrust of power had in the years since Independence been increasingly directed not only against the traditional rulers but also against the supposed representatives of the people, who now seemed to many to be often as distant and unrepresentative of the people's interest as Parliament once had been. "The representatives of the people, in a popular assembly," said Hamilton, in a typical Federalist belittling of the state legislatures, "seem sometimes to fancy that they are the people themselves."[172]

Many Americans seized on the people's growing suspicion of their own representatives and reversed the perspective: the houses of representatives, now no more trusted than other parts of the government, seemed to be also no more representative of the people than the other parts of the government. They had lost their exclusive role of embodying the people in the government. In fact the people did not actually participate in the government anymore, as they did, for example, in the English House of Commons. The Americans had taken the people out of the government altogether. The "true distinction" of the American governments, wrote Madison in *The Federalist*, "lies *in the total exclusion of the people, in their collective capacity*, from any share" in the government.[173]

Or from a different point of view the Americans could now argue that the people participated in all branches of the government and not merely in their houses of representatives. "The whole powers of the proposed government," said Hamilton in *The Federalist*, "is to be in the hands of the representatives of the people." All parts of the government were equally responsible but limited spokesmen for the people, who remained as the absolute and perpetual sovereign, distributing to their various agents bits and pieces of power that were out, so to speak, on temporary, always recallable loan.[174]

The American governments, wrote Samuel Williams in his *Natural and Civil History of Vermont* of 1794, "do not admit of sovereignty, nobility, or any kind of hereditary powers; but only of powers granted by the people, ascertained by written constitutions, and exercised by representation for a given time." Hence such governments "do not admit of monarchy, or aristocracy; nor do they admit of what was called democracy by the ancients." The old classification of politics by the number and character of the rulers into monarchy, aristocracy, and democracy—the classification that went back thousands of years—no longer made sense of American practice, where "all is transacted by representation" expressed in different ways. The government in the several states thus "varies in its form; committing more or less power to a governor, senate, or house of representatives, as the circumstances of any particular state may require. As each of these branches derive their whole power from the people, are accountable to them for the use and exercise they made of it, and may be displaced by the election of others," the liberty and security of the people, as Americans had thought in 1776, no longer came from their participation in one part of the government, as the democracy balanced against the monarchy and the aristocracy, "but from the responsibility, and dependence of each part of the government upon the people."[175]

In slightly more than two decades of polemics the Americans had destroyed the age-old conception of mixed or balanced government and had found new explanations for their polities created in 1776, explanations that rested on their expansion of the principle of representation. America had not discovered the idea of representation, said Madison, but it could "claim the merit of making the discovery the basis of unmixed and extensive republics."[176] And their republics were now peculiarly unmixed, despite the presence of senates and governors. They could in fact intelligibly be considered to be democracies, since, as James Wilson said, "in a democracy" the supreme power "is inherent in the people, and is either exercised by themselves or their representatives."[177]

Perhaps no one better described the "new and rich discoveries in jurisprudence" Americans had made than Wilson. The British constitution, said this underappreciated founder, who would be soon be appointed associate justice of the Supreme Court in the new national government, had attempted to combine and to balance the three different forms of government, but it had obviously failed. And it was left to the Americans to realize that it was "not necessary to intermix the different species of government" in order to attain perfection in politics. "We have discovered, that one of them—the best and purest—that, in which the supreme power remains with the people at large, is capable of being formed, arranged, proportioned, and organized in such a manner, as to exclude the inconveniences, and to secure the advantages of all three."[178] The Federal Constitution, said Wilson, was therefore "purely democratical," even though in its outward form it resembled the conventional mixed government: "all authority of every kind is *derived* by REPRESENTATION *from the* PEOPLE *and the* DEMOCRATIC *principle is carried into every part of the government.*" The new government was in fact, incongruous as it sounded, a mixed or balanced democracy.[179]

The Americans had reversed in a revolutionary way the traditional conception of politics: the stability of government no longer relied, as it had since antiquity, upon the embodiment in the government of the basic social forces of the state. Americans had retained the forms of the Aristotelian schemes of government but had eliminated the substance; they had divested the various parts of a mixed government of their social constituents. Institutional or governmental politics was abstracted from its former identity with the society, but at the same time a more modern and more realistic sense of political behavior in the society itself, among the people and their varying interests, could now be appreciated. The idea of classical politics, the politics of Aristotle and his successors, that involved balancing the three simple forms of government now no longer made sense in America. Most American theorists (but not John

Adams) would cease to talk about politics as the maneuverings among three estates of the society, among the one, the few, and the many.

Americans had begun the Revolution assuming that the people were a homogeneous entity set against the other orders in society and represented exclusively in the houses of representatives. But such an assumption belied American experience, and it took only a few years of independence to convince the best American minds that distinctions in the society, as Madison said, were "various and unavoidable," so much so that they could not be embodied in the government.[180] Once the people were thought to be composed of various interests in opposition to one another, all sense of a graduated organic chain in a homogeneous social hierarchy became irrelevant.

This change was symbolized by the increasing emphasis on the image of a Lockean social contract that replaced the Whig contract, legal or mercantile in character, that the colonists had imagined existing between rulers and ruled—equal parties with equal sets of rights—in which protection and allegiance were the considerations. Conceiving of this earlier Whig contract between the king and the people was the only way the colonists could justify their obeying the prerogative decrees and edicts of the king. "Allegiance," wrote James Wilson in 1774, "is the faith and obedience, which every subject owes to his prince. This obedience is founded on the protection derived from government: for protection and allegiance are the reciprocal bonds, which connect the prince and his subjects." This allegiance was not the same as consent. "Allegiance to the king and obedience to the parliament," said Wilson, "are founded on very different principles. The former is founded on protection:

the latter on representation. An inattention to this difference," said Wilson, "has produced...much uncertainty and confusion in our ideas concerning the connexion, which ought to subsist between Great Britain and the American colonies."[181]

Under the new system of American politics there was no place any longer for allegiance and protection and for the older idea of a contract between king and people. Consent was now the only basis for obedience to the laws and edicts of government, making all the officers of government in some sense representatives of the people. Instead of the older outmoded contract between rulers and ruled, Americans now stressed the contract among the people themselves, which was the contract that John Locke had emphasized. The people were not an organic estate or social order, which needed to bargain with its rulers, but rather an agglomeration of competitive individuals who came together and contracted for their mutual benefit to form a society; unlike the English Crown, the American governments possessed no independent existence with which the people needed to contract.

As Joel Barlow noted in 1792, the word *people* in America had taken on a different meaning from what it had in Europe. In Europe, said Barlow, the people were "something...difficult to define."[182] They were only a portion of the society; they were the poor, the *canaille,* the rabble, the miserables, the *menu peuple,* the *Pöbel.* But in America the people were not a fragment of the society and not the lowest stratum of the society; they had become the whole society and were taking on a quasi-sacred character. "Society," said Enos Hitchcock in 1788, "is composed of individuals—they are parts of the whole."[183] And such individuals in America were the entire society: there could be nothing else—no orders, no lords, no monarch, no magistrates in the traditional sense of the term.

"Without the distinctions of titles, families, or nobility," wrote Samuel Williams, "they acknowledged and reverenced only those distinctions which nature had made, in a diversity of talents, abilities, and virtues. There were no family interests, connexions, or estates, large enough to oppress them. There was no excessive wealth in the hands of a few, sufficient to corrupt them." The Americans were thus both equal and unequal at the same time. "They all feel that nature has made them equal in respect to their rights;" said Williams, "or rather that nature has given to them a common and an equal right to liberty, to property and to safety; to justice, government, laws, religion, and freedom. They all see that nature has made them very unequal in respect to their original powers, capacities, and talents. They become united in claiming and in preserving the equality, which nature has assigned to them; and in availing themselves of the benefits, which are designed, and may be derived from the inequality, which nature has also established."[184]

Politics in such a society could no longer be simply described as a contest between rulers and people, or between institutionalized orders or estates of the society. The political struggles would in fact be among the people themselves, among all the various groups and individuals seeking to create inequality out of their equality by gaining control of an autonomous government divested of its former identity with the society.

It was this disembodiment of government from society that ultimately made possible the conception of modern politics and the eventual justification of competing parties among the people. Those who criticized such divisive jealousy and opposition among the people, said William Hornby of South Carolina in 1784, did not understand "the great change in politics, which the revolution must have necessarily produced. . . . In *these* days we are equal citizens of a DEMOCRATIC REPUBLIC, in which *jealousy* and *opposition* must naturally exist, while there exists a difference in the minds, interests, and sentiments of mankind."[185]

Although few were as yet willing to justify factionalism and parties so blatantly, many now realized with Madison that "the regulation of these various and interfering interests forms the principal task of modern legislation, and involves the spirit of party and faction in the necessary and ordinary operations of the government."[186] Legislation in such a society could not be the transcending of the different interests but the reconciling of them. Despite Madison's lingering hope, the public good could not be an entity distinct from its parts; it was rather, as one Carolinian put it, "the general combined interest of all the state put together, as it were, upon an average."[187]

Such language was recognizably modern. Indeed, it was this intellectual emergence into modernity that marked the revolutionary generation's contribution to politics. Many old attitudes died hard, and the implications of many new ideas still had to be followed out; but the essential breakthrough into a new understanding of politics had been made. While others in the early nineteenth century would soon follow the Americans' course, driven not by example but by similar kinds of political and intellectual pressures, the American revolutionaries could rightly claim that they had been the first people to transcend the classical paradigm of politics. "As this kind of government," wrote

Samuel Williams, "is not the same as that, which has been called monarchy, aristocracy, or democracy; as it had a conspicuous origin in America, and has not been suffered to prevail in any other part of the globe, it would be no more than just and proper, to distinguish it by its proper name, and call it, *The American System of Government.*"[188]

It was an extraordinary intellectual achievement, ultimately made possible by the substantial changes that had taken place in American society and politics, and yet at the same time made comprehensible by changes that had taken place in the conception of representation. Representation became both the measure and the means of the Americans' creating a new system of politics and a new understanding of democracy. It was "the introduction of this new principle of representative democracy," Jefferson later remarked, that "rendered useless almost everything written before on the structure of government; and, in a great measure, relieves our regret, if the political writings of Aristotle, or of any other ancient, have been lost, or are unfaithfully rendered or explained to us."[189] The discussion of politics would never again be the same.

Notes

1. Jefferson to Thomas Nelson, May 16, 1776, in *The Papers of Thomas Jefferson,* ed. Julian P. Boyd et al. (Princeton, 1950–), 1:292.

2. [Thomas Whateley], *The Regulations Lately Made concerning the Colonies and the Taxes Imposed upon Them, Considered* (London, 1765), 108; [Soame Jenyns], *The Objections to the Taxation of Our American Colonies, by the Legislatures of Great Britain, Briefly Consider'd* (London, 1765), 7.

3. [Whateley], *Regulations,* 112.

4. [Jenyns], *Objections,* 8–9.

5. [Whateley], *Regulations,* 109.

6. [Jenyns], *Objections,* 8.

7. Burke, "Speech to the Electors of Bristol" (1774), in *The Works of the Right Honorable Edmund Burke* (Boston, 1865–71), 2:96.

8. William Blackstone, *Commentaries on the Laws of England* (Oxford, 1765–69), 1:159.

9. [Whateley], *Regulations,* 109.

10. [Whateley], *Regulations,* 109.

11. [Daniel Dulany], *Considerations on the Propriety of Imposing Taxes in the British Colonies…* ([Annapolis, MD], 1765), in *Pamphlets of the American Revolution, 1750–1776,* ed. Bernard Bailyn (Cambridge, MA, 1965), 1:611.

12. Benjamin Church, *Oration, Delivered at Boston, March 5, 1773,* in *Principles and Acts of the Revolution in America,* ed. Hezekiah

Niles (New York, 1876), 36; Maurice Moore, *The Justice and Policy of Taxing the American Colonies...* (Wilmington, NC, 1765), in *Some Eighteenth-Century Tracts concerning North Carolina,* ed. William K. Boyd (Raleigh, NC, 1927), 167.

13. Declaration of the Stamp Act Congress (Oct. 19, 1765), in *American Colonial Documents to 1776,* ed. Merrill Jensen (New York, 1962), 672.

14. Moore, *The Justice and Policy of Taxing the American Colonies,* 169.

15. [Dulany], *Considerations on the Propriety of Imposing Taxes,* 1:612.

16. Phila. *Pennsylvania Packet,* June 12, 1775, Dec. 19, 1774.

17. [Moses Mather], *America's Appeal to the Impartial World* (Hartford, 1775), 14.

18. Phila. *Pennsylvania Packet,* Dec. 19, 1774.

19. [Dickinson], "Letters of a Farmer in Pennsylvania," in *The Life and Writings of John Dickinson,* ed. Paul L. Ford, Memoirs of the Historical Society of Pennsylvania 14 (Philadelphia, 1895), 2:348–50. On the new conception of the empire, see Richard Koebner, *Empire* (Cambridge, MA, 1961), 168–69, 211–15; Randolph Adams, *Political Ideas of the American Revolution* (Durham, NC, 1922), 64–85.

20. Moore, *The Justice and Policy of Taxing the American Colonies,* 167.

21. [Richard Wells], *The Middle Line; or, An Attempt to Furnish Some Hints for Ending the Differences Subsisting between Great Britain and the Colonies* (Philadelphia, 1775), 29.

22. Samuel West, *A Sermon Preached... in New-England, May 29th, 1776* (Boston, 1776), in *The Pulpit of the American Revolution: or, The Political Sermons of the Period of 1776,* ed. John W. Thornton (Boston, 1860), 280; Address by Gouverneur Morris in the New York Convention, 1777, in Jared Sparks, *The Life of Gouverneur Morris* (Boston, 1832), 1:107; Charleston *Gazette of the State of South Carolina,* June 20, 1774.

23. Lee to Hannah Corbin, Mar. 17, 1778, in *The Letters of Richard Henry Lee,* ed. James C. Ballagh (New York, 1911), 1:393.

24. [Alexander Hamilton], *The Farmer Refuted...* (New York, 1775), in *The Papers of Alexander Hamilton,* ed. Harold C. Syrett and Jacob E. Cooke (New York, 1961–), 1:100.

25. [Mather], *America's Appeal,* 14.

26. [Hamilton], *The Farmer Refuted,* 1:96–97, 100, 105–7.

27. Lee to Hannah Corbin, Mar. 17, 1778, in *Letters of Richard Henry*

Lee, 1:393. On the revolutionaries' acceptance of the concept of virtual representation, see Richard Buel Jr., "Democracy and the American Revolution: A Frame of Reference," *William and Mary Quarterly,* 3d ser., 21 (1964): 169–90.

28. [Wells], *The Middle Line,* 30–31.

29. Boston *Independent Chronicle,* Apr. 3, July 10, 1777.

30. *Providence Gazette,* Apr. 3, 1779.

31. Boston *Independent Chronicle,* July 10, 1777. See also Trenton *New Jersey Gazette,* Jan. 7, 1778, in *Documents Relating to the Revolutionary History of the State of New Jersey,* ed. Francis B. Lee (Trenton, 1903), 2:2–3.

32. [Adams], *Thoughts on Government* (Philadelphia, 1776), in *The Works of John Adams,* ed. Charles Francis Adams (Boston, 1850–56), 4:194–95. See also the Worcester *Massachusetts Spy,* July 12 and 26, 1775.

33. Watchman, *To the Inhabitants of the City and County of New York,* Apr. 15, 1776 (New York, 1776).

34. Essay, Philadelphia, June 22, 1774, in *American Archives,* ed. Peter Force, 4th ser. (Washington, DC, 1837–56), 1:441.

35. Otis, *Considerations on Behalf of the Colonists . . .* (London, 1765), in *Some Political Writings of James Otis,* ed. Charles F. Mullett, University of Missouri Studies 4 (Columbia, MO, 1929), 359, 366.

36. Church, *Oration, 1773,* in Niles, *Principles and Acts of the Revolution,* 36.

37. Moore, *The Justice and Policy of Taxing the American Colonies,* in Boyd, *Some Eighteenth-Century Tracts,* 169.

38. [John Joachim Zubly], *An Humble Enquiry into the Nature of the Dependency of the American Colonies* (Charleston, SC, 1769), 17, 22.

39. Boston *Evening Post,* June 24, 1765.

40. Adams to James Sullivan, May 26, 1776, in *Works of John Adams,* 9:375. On the problem of suffrage during the Revolution, see Chilton Williamson, *American Suffrage: From Property to Democracy, 1760–1860* (Princeton, 1960), 76–116; and Alexander Keyssar, *The Right to Vote: The Contested History of Democracy in the United States* (New York, 2000), 8–25.

41. Phila. *Pennsylvania Gazette,* May 15, 1776; Boston *Independent Chronicle,* Apr. 9, 1778, Sept. 23, 1779; Boston *Continental Journal,* Jan. 8, 1778.

42. [Hamilton], *The Farmer Refuted*, in *Papers of Alexander Hamilton*, 1:105; *The Triumph of the Whigs: or T'Other Congress Convened* (New York, 1775), 8.

43. Essay, Philadelphia, June 22, 1774, in Force, *American Archives*, 1:442.

44. See, e.g., Charles S. Grant, *Democracy in the Connecticut Frontier Town of Kent* (New York, 1961), 115–16.

45. Jack P. Greene, *The Quest for Power: The Lower Houses of Assembly in the Southern Royal Colonies, 1689–1776* (Chapel Hill, 1963), 384.

46. Boston *Continental Journal*, Jan. 8, 1778.

47. New York Constitution (1777), Art. XVI.

48. Bernard Bailyn, *The Ideological Origins of the American Revolution* (Cambridge, MA, 1967), 162–64.

49. [Zubly], *Humble Enquiry*, 17. See in general Hubert Phillips, *The Development of a Residential Qualification for Representatives in Colonial Legislatures* (Cincinnati, 1921). The medieval and early modern origins and development of English representation can be traced in a voluminous literature on the subject, including M. V. Clarke, *Medieval Representation and Consent* (London, 1936); Charles H. McIlwain, "Medieval Estates," *Cambridge Medieval History* (1932), 7:665–715; J. G. Edwards, "The Plena Potestas of English Parliamentary Representation," in *Oxford Essays in Medieval History, Presented to Herbert Edward Salter* (Oxford, 1934), 141–54; Edwards, "Taxation and Consent in the Court of Common Pleas," *English Historical Review* 57 (1942): 473–78; Gaines Post, "Plena Potestas and Consent in Medieval Assemblies: A Study in Romano-Canonical Procedure and the Rise of Representation, 1150–1325," *Traditio* 1 (1943): 355–408; G. O. Sayles, "Representation of Cities and Boroughs in 1268," *English Historical Review* 40 (1925): 580–85; Helen M. Cam, "The Relation of English Members of Parliament to Their Constituencies in the Fourteenth Century," in *Liberties and Communities in Medieval England*, ed. Cam (Cambridge, Eng., 1944), 223–35; Cam, "The Legislators of Medieval England," *Proceedings of the British Academy* 31 (1945): 127–50; T. F. T. Plucknett, "The Lancasterian Constitution," in *Tudor Studies Presented . . . to A. E. Pollard* (London, 1924); S. B. Chrimes, *English Constitutional Ideas in the Fifteenth Century* (Cambridge, Eng., 1936), 66–101, 115–26; Edward

T. Lampson, "Some New Light on the Growth of Parliamentary Sovereignty: Wimbash versus Tallebois," *American Political Science Review* 35 (1941): 952–60. On the eighteenth-century English conceptions, see Samuel H. Beer, "The Representation of Interests in British Government: Historical Background," *American Political Science Review* 51 (1957): 613–50.

50. Lee to Hannah Corbin, Mar. 17, 1778, in *Letters of Richard Henry Lee,* 1:391.

51. Phila. *Pennsylvania Journal,* Mar. 8, 1775; Delaware Declaration of Rights (1776), VI; Maryland Declaration of Rights (1776), V.

52. Boston's Instructions to Its Representatives, May 30, 1776, in *The Popular Sources of Political Authority: Documents on the Massachusetts Constitution of 1780,* ed. Oscar Handlin and Mary Handlin (Cambridge, MA, 1966), 95.

53. "Loose Thoughts on Government" (1776), in Force, *American Archives,* 6:730.

54. Boston's Instructions to Its Representatives, May 30, 1776, in Handlin and Handlin, *Popular Sources of Political Authority,* 95.

55. Albemarle County Instructions concerning the Virginia Constitution (1776), in *Papers of Thomas Jefferson,* 6:287.

56. Boston *Massachusetts Spy,* Feb. 16, 1775.

57. [Mather], *America's Appeal,* 70.

58. Phillips Payson, *A Sermon Preached… at Boston, May 17, 1778,* in Thornton, *Pulpit of the American Revolution,* 330.

59. Adams, Notes for an Oration at Braintree, Spring, 1772, in *Diary and Autobiography of John Adams,* ed. Lyman H. Butterfield et al. (Cambridge, MA, 1961), 2:57–62.

60. [Daniel Leonard], *Address to the Inhabitants of the Province of Massachusetts Bay, Jan. 9, 1775,* in John Adams and [Daniel Leonard], *Novanglus and Massachusettensis* (Boston, 1819), 169.

61. Adams, Notes for an Oration at Braintree, in *Diary and Autobiography of John Adams,* 2:58, 60. On mixed government, see also Blackstone, *Commentaries on Law,* 1:48; John Witherspoon, "Lectures on Moral Philosophy," in the *The Works of John Witherspoon* (Philadelphia, 1800), 3:334–38. For historians' discussion of the theory of mixed or balanced government, see Stanley Pargellis, "The Theory of Balanced Government," in *The Constitution Reconsidered,* ed. Conyers Read (New York, 1958), 37–49; Leonard W. Labaree, *Conservatism in Early American History*

(New York, 1948), 119–41; Bailyn, *Ideological Origins of the American Revolution*, 70–77, 273–80; Gordon S. Wood, *The Creation of the American Republic, 1776–1787* (Chapel Hill, 1969). On the origins and development of the theory of the mixed English constitution, especially the seventeenth-century transformation of the monarchy into one of three estates of the realm, see Corinne C. Weston, *English Constitutional Theory and the House of Lords, 1556–1832* (New York, 1965), chaps. 1–4.

62. Pendleton, quoted in Margaret V. Smith, *Virginia, 1492–1892,… with a History of the Executives… of Virginia* (Washington, DC, 1893), 214.

63. New York *Journal,* Dec. 11, 1766. Montesquieu, of course, was the most famous eighteenth-century exponent of the relation between cultural traits and forms of government.

64. On the representational basis of parliamentary sovereignty, see Lampson, "Some New Light on the Growth of Parliamentary Sovereignty"; J. W. Gough, *Fundamental Law in English Constitutional History* (Oxford, 1961), 25–27, 80–97.

65. Adams, *Defence of the Constitutions of the United States* (1787–88), in *Works of John Adams,* 4:300.

66. William Hooper, Address to the North Carolina Congress, Oct. 26, 1776, in *Colonial Records of North Carolina,* ed. William L. Saunders (Raleigh, 1886–90), 10:867.

67. Adams, Notes for an Oration at Braintree, in *Diary and Autobiography of John Adams,* 2:58.

68. James Burgh, *Political Disquisitions* (London, 1774–75), 1:8–9, 12–14.

69. Zera Fink, *The Classical Republicans: An Essay in the Recovery of a Pattern of Thought in Seventeenth Century England* (Evanston, IL, 1945), 102–3, 109–10.

70. Josiah Tucker, *The True Interest of Britain Set Forth in Regard to the Colonies…* (Philadelphia, 1776), 26; Phila. *Pennsylvania Packet,* Sept. 4, 1775.

71. Richard A. Ryerson, *The Revolution Is Now Begun: The Radical Committees of Philadelphia, 1765–1776* (Philadelphia, 1978), 66, 31; Edward Countryman, *A People in Revolution: The American Revolution and Political Society in New York, 1760–1790* (Baltimore, 1981), 125; Staughton Lynd, *Class Conflict, Slavery, and the United States Constitution: Ten Essays* (Indianapolis, 1968),

79–108; Charles S. Olton, *Artisans for Independence: Philadelphia Mechanics and the American Revolution* (Syracuse, 1975), 55; Richard W. Walsh, *Charleston's Sons of Liberty: A Study of the Artisans, 1763–1787* (Columbia, SC, 1959), 27.

72. Ryerson, *Revolution Is Now Begun,* 32–33, 47, 50, 73, 75; Kenneth Coleman, *The American Revolution in Georgia, 1763–1789* (Athens, GA, 1958), 63.

73. New York *Gazette,* Apr. 4, 1765, New York *Journal,* Dec. 21, 1769, quoted in Bernard Friedman, "The Shaping of the Radical Consciousness in Provincial New York," *Journal of American History* 56 (1970): 789–90, 793–94; Olton, *Artisans for Independence,* 52.

74. William Henry Drayton, *The Letters of Freeman, Etc.: Essays on the Nonimportation Movement in South Carolina,* ed. Robert M. Weir (Columbia, SC, 1977), 31.

75. Thomas Rodney to Caesar Rodney, May 26, 1776, in *Letters to and from Caesar Rodney, 1756–1784,* ed. George H. Ryden (Philadelphia, 1933), 84.

76. On the broadening of instructions into areas of general public policy during the Revolution, see J. R. Pole, *Political Representation in England and the Origins of the American Republic* (New York, 1966), 72–73. For the novel use of instructions in North Carolina, see Elisha P. Douglass, *Rebels and Democrats: The Struggle for Equal Political Rights and Majority Rule during the American Revolution* (Chapel Hill, 1955), 115. Virginia experienced a rash of county instructions in 1776 over the issue of religion. *Papers of Thomas Jefferson,* 1:525–29.

77. Charleston *Gazette of the State of South Carolina,* Aug. 19, July 17, 1784.

78. [Anon.], *Rudiments of Law and Government, Deduced from the Law of Nature*... (Charleston, SC, 1783), 33–34; Burke, "Speech to the Electors of Bristol" (1774), in *Works,* 2:96.

79. [William Whiting], *An Address to the Inhabitants of the County of Berkshire*... (Hartford, 1778), 24.

80. Boston *Independent Chronicle,* June 11, 1778.

81. [Levi Hart], *The Description of Good Character*... (Hartford, [1786]), 16.

82. Phila. *Pennsylvania Packet,* Sept. 15, 1786.

83. Trenton *New Jersey Gazette,* Jan. 7, 1778, in Lee, *Documents Relating to the Revolutionary History of New Jersey,* 2:2.

84. Boston *Independent Chronicle,* Mar. 23, 1780.

85. Instructions of Mecklenburg and Orange Counties, 1776, in Saunders, *Colonial Records of North Carolina,* 10:870 b,f.

86. Elbridge Gerry to James Warren, June 25, 1776, in *Letters of Members of the Continental Congress,* ed. Edmund Burnett (Washington, DC, 1921–36). On this separation between the people and their representatives, see also Maryland Delegates to Council of Safety, June 11, 1776, in Force, *American Archives,* 6:806–7; Herbert E. Klingelhofer, "The Cautious Revolution: Maryland and the Movement toward Independence, Part I," *Maryland Historical Magazine* 40 (1965): 305.

87. Jefferson, Notes of Proceedings in the Continental Congress, June 7–Aug. 1, 1776, in *Papers of Thomas Jefferson,* 1:312.

88. Albemarle County Instructions concerning the Virginia Constitution (1776), in *Papers of Thomas Jefferson,* 6:286–87.

89. Address of the Mechanics of New York City, June 14, 1776, in Niles, *Principles and Acts of the Revolution,* 174–76.

90. Phila. *Pennsylvania Journal,* Mar. 12, 1776.

91. Phila. *Pennsylvania Packet,* Oct. 5, 1776.

92. [Benjamin Austin], *Observations on the Pernicious Practice of the Law* (Boston, 1786), 44–45.

93. [Anon.], *Rudiments of Law and Government,* 33.

94. [Noah Webster], "Government," *American Magazine* 1 (1787–88): 207.

95. [Benjamin Rush], *Observations upon the Present Government of Pennsylvania* (Philadelphia, 1777), in *The Selected Writings of Benjamin Rush,* ed. Dagobert D. Runes (New York, 1947), 71.

96. Boston *Independent Chronicle,* Jan. 18, 1787.

97. Benjamin Hichborn, *An Oration, Delivered July 5th, 1784* (Boston, [1784]), 13.

98. Hartford *Connecticut Courant,* Oct. 21, 1783.

99. Samuel McClintock, *A Sermon Preached . . . June 3, 1784* (Portsmouth, 1784), 43.

100. Moses Mather, *Sermon Preached in the Audience of the General Assembly of the State of Connecticut . . . May 10, 1781* (New London, 1781), 11; [David Cooper], *An Enquiry into Public Abuses, Arising for Want of a Due Execution of the Laws* (Philadelphia, 1784), 3.

101. Henry Cummings, *A Sermon Preached before His Honor Thomas*

    Cushing...May 18, 1783 (Boston, 1783), 13; McClintock, *Sermon,* 43; Samuel Wales, *A Sermon Preached before the General Assembly of the State of Connecticut...May 12th, 1785* (Hartford, 1785), 21.

102. Zabdiel Adams, *A Sermon Preached before...John Hancock...May 29, 1782* (Boston, [1782]), 25; Boston *Independent Chronicle,* Dec. 1, 1785; Charleston *South Carolina Gazette and General Advertiser,* May 11–13, 1784.

103. Baltimore *Maryland Journal,* Apr. 13, 1787.

104. Baltimore *Maryland Journal,* Feb. 2 and 6, 1787. Some of the writings on the Maryland debate have been collected and published in Melvin Yazawa, ed., *Representative Government and the Revolution: The Maryland Consitutional Crisis of 1787* (Baltmore, 1975).

105. Baltimore *Maryland Journal,* Feb. 13, Jan. 23, Feb. 13, 1787.

106. Baltimore *Maryland Journal,* Nov. 8, 1785, May 1, 1787.

107. Baltimore *Maryland Journal,* Apr. 6, Feb. 23, May 1, 1787.

108. Baltimore *Maryland Journal,* Feb. 23, 1787.

109. Baltimore *Maryland Journal,* June 22, Aug. 3, 1787.

110. Baltimore *Maryland Journal,* Feb. 13 and 20, May 18, Aug. 31, 1787. James Burgh used the image of the sun and moon in his *Political Disquisitions; or, An Enquiry into Public Errors, Defects, and Abuses* (Philadelphia, 1775), 1:3–4.

111. Baltimore *Maryland Journal,* Feb. 15, May 10 and 18, Aug. 31, 1787.

112. Baltimore *Maryland Journal,* Feb. 13, 1787.

113. Baltimore *Maryland Journal,* Aug. 3, May 1, 1787.

114. Baltimore *Maryland Journal,* Apr. 13, 1787.

115. "Loose Thoughts on Government" (1776), in Force, *American Archives,* 6:731.

116. [Rush], *Observations upon the Present Government of Pennsylvania,* in *Selected Writings of Benjamin Rush,* 68.

117. Hartford *Connecticut Courant,* Apr. 2, 1787.

118. Boston *Independent Chronicle,* Dec. 19, 1782, Jan. 16, 1783.

119. Frederick Muhlenberg, quoted in Oswald Seidensticker, "Frederick Augustus Conrad Muhlenberg, Speaker of the House of Representatives, in the first Congress, 1789," *Pennsylvania Magazine of History and Biography,* 13 (1889): 184, 199–200. For the reapportionment decisions of the Supreme Court in the 1960s, see *Baker v. Carr* (1962) and *Reynolds v. Sims* (1964).

120. [Thomas Tudor Tucker], *Conciliatory Hints, Attempting by a Fair State of Matters to Remove Party Prejudice...* (Charleston, SC, 1784), 25.

121. [Tucker], *Conciliatory Hints,* 25–26.

122. Gouverneur Morris, in *The Records of the Federal Convention in 1787,* ed. Max Farrand (New Haven, 1911, 1937), 1:522.

123. Hartford *Connecticut Courant,* Nov. 27, 1786, Feb. 5, 1787; James Wilson, in Farrand, *Records of the Federal Convention,* 1:253.

124. James Madison's Observations on Jefferson's Draft of a Constitution for Virginia (1788), in *Papers of Thomas Jefferson,* 6:308.

125. [Madison], *The Federalist,* No. 10; James Wilson, in Farrand, *Records of the Federal Convention,* 1:253.

126. James Madison, Vices of the Political System of the United States (1787), in *The Papers of James Madison,* ed. Robert Rutland et al. (Charlottesville, 1975), 9:357.

127. James Wilson, in Farrand, *Records of the Federal Convention,* 1:253; [Madison], *The Federalist,* No. 10.

128. For an extended discussion of the social and political consequences of an expanded electorate, see [William Pitt Beers], *An Address to the Legislature and People of the State of Connecticut...* (New Haven, 1791), 18–23. On the emergence of obscure men into politics during the Revolution, see Jackson Turner Main, "Government by the People: The American Revolution and the Democratization of the Legislatures," *William and Mary Quarterly,* 3d ser., 23 (1966): 391–407, and his *The Upper House in Revolutionary America, 1763–1788* (Madison, WI, 1967).

129. Samuel Chase, quoted in Phillip A. Crowl, "Anti-Federalism in Maryland, 1787–1788," *William and Mary Quarterly,* 3d ser., 4 (1947): 446, 464.

130. "Address and Reasons of Dissent of the Minority of the Convention of the State of Pennsylvania," Dec. 18, 1787, in *Pennsylvania and the Federal Constitution, 1787–1788,* ed. John B. McMaster and Frederick D. Stone (Philadelphia, 1888), 472.

131. William Heath (MA), Robert Lansing (NY), Melancthon Smith (NY), and Patrick Henry (VA), in *The Debates in the Several State Conventions, on the Adoption of the Federal Constitution,* ed. Jonathan Elliot (Washington, DC, 1854), 2:13, 293, 247, 260, 3:54.

132. [Melancthon Smith?], *Observations Leading to a Fair Examination of the System of Government, Proposed by the Late Conven-*

tion... in a Numbers of Letters from the Federal Farmer ([New York], 1787, in *Pamphlets on the Constitution of the United States,* ed. Paul L. Ford (Brooklyn, 1888), 295; "Address and Reasons of Dissent," in McMaster and Stone, *Pennsylvania and the Federal Constitution,* 471; R. H. Lee to Edmund Randolph, Oct. 16, 1787, in *Letters of Richard Henry Lee,* 2:452.

133. "Address and Reasons of Dissent," in McMaster and Stone, *Pennsylvania and the Federal Constitution,* 471.

134. Melancthon Smith (NY), in Elliot, *Debates,* 2:246.

135. Boston *Independent Chronicle,* Dec. 13, 1787; [Smith?], *Observations,* in Ford, *Pamphlets on the Constitution,* 295.

136. Samuel Chase, quoted in Crowl, "Anti-Federalism in Maryland," 446, 464.

137. On the intense localism of the Anti-Federalists, see Cecelia M. Kenyon, "Men of Little Faith: The Anti-Federalists on the Nature of Representative Government," *William and Mary Quarterly,* 3d ser., 12 (1955): 3–43; and Saul Cornell, *The Other Founders: Anti-Federalism and the Dissenting Tradition in America, 1788–1828* (Chapel Hill, 1999).

138. Farrand, *Records of the Federal Convention,* 2:278.

139. Elliot, *Debates,* 2:256.

140. J. C. Jones (MA), Samuel Stillman (MA), John Marshall (VA), Samuel Johnson (NC), and Edmund Pendleton (VA), in Elliot, *Debates,* 2:29, 167, 3:233, 4:56, 3:299–300.

141. [Dickinson], The Letters of Fabius, in 1788, on the Federal Constitution (Wilmington, DE, 1787), in Ford, *Pamphlets on the Constitution,* 178.

142. [Tench Coxe], *An Examination of the Constitution for the United States* (Philadelphia, 1788), in Ford, *Pamphlets on the Constitution,* 147.

143. [James Iredell], *Answers to Mr. Mason's Objections to the New Constitution* (Newburn, NC, 1788), in Ford, *Pamphlets on the Constitution,* 340; Hamilton, in Elliot, *Debates,* 2:253.

144. Nathaniel Chipman, *Sketches of the Principles of Government* (Rutland, 1793), 150.

145. [William Vans Murray], *Political Sketches, Inscribed to His Excellency John Adams* (London, 1787), 52–53.

146. [John Stevens], *Observations on Government* (New York, 1787), 31.

147. James Wilson, "Lectures on Law Delivered in the College

of Philadelphia in the Years 1790–1791," in *The Works of James Wilson,* ed. Robert G. McCloskey (Cambridge, MA, 1967), 1:445. By 1823 Jefferson, who in 1776 in his desire to establish an aristocratic senate free from popular dictation had been willing to have it elected for life, was suggesting to European constitution makers that in order "to avoid all temptation to superior pretensions of the one over the other House, and the possibility of either erecting itself into a privileged order, might it not be better to choose at the same time and in the same mode, a body sufficiently numerous to be divided by lot into two separate Houses, acting as independently as the two Houses in England, or in our governments, and to shuffle their names together, and redistribute them by lot, once a week for a fortnight?" Jefferson to A. Coray, Oct. 31, 1823, in *The Writings of Thomas Jefferson,* ed. Andrew A. Lipscomb and Albert E. Bergh (Washington, DC, 1905), 15:485–86.

148. Wilson, "Lectures on Law," in *Works of James Wilson,* 1:398–99.

149. *Providence Gazette,* May 12, 1787.

150. [Hamilton], *The Federalist,* No. 78.

151. John Leland, quoted in William A. Robinson, *Jeffersonian Democracy in New England* (New Haven, 1916), 120.

152. Henry Lee (VA), in Elliot, *Debates,* 3:177.

153. Chipman, *Sketches of the Principles of Government,* 239, 277.

154. [Murray], *Political Sketches,* 1.

155. Paine, *The Rights of Man* (London, 1791), in *The Complete Writings of Thomas Paine,* ed. Phillip S. Foner (New York, 1945), 1:354.

156. [Murray], *Political Sketches,* 5.

157. [Stevens], *Observations on Government,* 50.

158. Chipman, *Sketches of the Principles of Government,* 102.

159. [Madison], *The Federalist,* No. 10, No. 14.

160. Hamilton, Notes for a Speech of July 12, 1788, in the New York Ratifying Convention, in *Papers of Alexander Hamilton,* 5:105.

161. Paine, *Rights of Man,* 1:370–71. On the confusion of terms, see Robert W. Shoemaker, "'Democracy' and 'Republic' as Understood in Late Eighteenth-Century America," *American Speech* 61 (1966): 83–95.

162. [Madison], *The Federalist,* No. 10.

163. Samuel Williams, *The Natural and Civil History of Vermont* (Walpole, VT, 1794), 342.

164. Charles Pinckney (SC) and Edmund Randolph (VA), in Elliot, *Debates,* 4:331, 3:199.

165. Samuel Langdon, *The Republic of the Israelites an Example to the American States* (Exeter, NH, 1788), 9.

166. Wilson, in McMaster and Stone, *Pennsylvania and the Federal Constitution,* 222–23.

167. Williams, *Natural and Civil History of Vermont,* 343.

168. [Madison], *The Federalist,* No. 14.

169. Wilson, "Lectures on Law," in *Works of James Wilson,* 1:430, 2:57.

170. [Madison], *The Federalist,* No. 63.

171. Edmund Pendleton (VA), in Elliot, *Debates,* 3:301.

172. [Hamilton], *The Federalist,* No. 78.

173. [Madison], *The Federalist,* No. 71, No. 63.

174. [Hamilton], *The Federalist,* No. 28.

175. Williams, *Natural and Civil History of Vermont,* 342, 343.

176. [Madison], *The Federalist,* No. 14.

177. Wilson, in McMaster and Stone, *Pennsylvania and the Federal Constitution,* 230.

178. Wilson, "Lectures on Law," in *Works of James Wilson,* 1:416–17.

179. Wilson, in McMaster and Stone, *Pennsylvania and the Federal Constitution,* 231, 344.

180. Madison to Jefferson, Oct. 24, 1787, in *Papers of Thomas Jefferson,* 12:277.

181. James Wilson, *Considerations on the Authority of Parliament* (1774), in *Works of James Wilson,* 2:736–37.

182. Joel Barlow, *Advice to the Privileged Orders in the Several States of Europe* (London, 1792) (repr., Ithaca, NY, 1956), 17.

183. Enos Hitchcock, *An Oration Delivered July 4, 1788* (Providence, RI, [1788]), 18.

184. Williams, *Natural and Civil History of Vermont,* 344, 330.

185. Charleston *Gazette of the State of South Carolina,* July 29, 1784.

186. [Madison], *The Federalist,* No. 10.

187. Charleston *Gazette of the State of South Carolina,* July 17, 1784.

188. Williams, *Natural and Civil History of Vermont,* 346.

189. Jefferson to Isaac Tiffany, Aug. 26, 1816, in *Writings of Thomas Jefferson,* 15:66, 190.

Index

Continental Congress, 37

consent: different from allegiance, 78–79; explicitness of, 27; as foundation of government, 16; and voting, 29

constitution, Delaware, 21

constitution, English: and mixed government, 24, 25; representation in, 15, 71–72

Constitution, Federal: debate over, 54; as a democracy, 77; and elites, 57, 61; and a new conception of politics, 69, 77; and representation, 56; as "strictly republican," 62; mentioned, x, 2, 42, 53, 61

constitution, Maryland, 21

Constitutional Convention, 55, 59

constitutional conventions (state), 52, 74

constitutions, state: and democracy, 22; representation in, 13, 18; mentioned, 11

contract: Lockean, 78; Whig, 78

Coxe, Tench, 64

Creation of the American Republic, 1776–1787, ix

Crown, English, 72

Declaration of Independence, 33

Delaware, 20, 33

demagogues, 41

democracy: and American governments, 64–65, 70, 76; excluded from American governments, 49, 75; and federal Constitution, 59, 70, 77; and localism, 55, 56; James Madison on, 70; and mistrust of government, 30, 33; and mixed government, 22, 23, 24, 26, 48, 49; modern meaning of, 1, 70; perversion of, 23; and representation, 20, 49, 50; and state constitutions, 22

Dickinson, John, 10, 59–60, 63

disinterestedness, 12, 13, 32, 33, 61

Drayton, William Henry, 32

Dulany, Daniel, 8, 14

Dunwich (England), 5, 17

election: as the criterion of actual representation, 29, 47, 50; as incidental to virtual representation, 4, 26; of judges, x, 67–68; and representation, 26, 29, 47

Elton, G. R., ix

Electoral College, x

England, 9, 14

equality, 80

executive, as representative of the people, 65

federalism: Madison on, 73–74; mentioned, 2, 73

Federalists: and the Constitution, 61–62; and democracy, 68; on the judiciary, 66–68; on a new conception of politics, 68; on representation, 54, 55, 56, 59, 62, 63, 72, 74

Federalist, The, 57, 66–67, 70, 74, 75

Findley, William, 55

franchise, 4, 11. *See also* suffrage

Franklin, Benjamin, 9

ereignty, 24, 73; mentioned, 8,
9, 10, 15, 74. *See also* House of
Commons

parties, 81

Pendleton, Edmund, 24, 73

Pennsylvania: constitution of,
39; representation in, 36, 39,
50; mentioned, 10, 14, 18, 59

people: American, as whole society, 79; American, possessing
sovereignty, 73, 74, 75; English,
as homogeneous estate, 5, 12,
19, 28; as individuals, 79–80;
mistrust of government by,
28, 33, 38, 39; not homogeneous entity in America, 27,
79; remaining outside of all
government, 49, 51, 66, 75;
represented in all parts of
government, 50, 62, 63, 66,
72; represented exclusively
in houses of representatives,
26; as superior to all parts of
government, 36–37, 45, 46, 74

petitioning, contrasted with
instructions, 33

Philadelphia, 30

Pinckney, Charles, 71

Pole, J. R., ix

political theory: and American
Revolution, 69–70; and mixed
government, 22, 77–78; and
modernity, 81; new American
conception of, 27, 49, 68, 69,
75–76, 80–81; and representation, 1, 17, 49

politics: classical, 22, 23, 75, 77, 80,
81, 82; modern, 75, 77, 80–81

Polybius, 25

Progressive reformers, 74

property qualifications: for the
suffrage, 11; for the representatives, 13, 14

public good, 12, 22, 31, 33, 34, 35, 81

Randolph, Edmund, 71

ratification, popular, of constitutions, 74

recall, 74

referendums, x, 74

representation: in all parts of
America's governments,
48, 49, 51, 52, 63–67, 75–76;
American confusion over, 20;
and Anti-Federalists, 58; as
basis of American system of
government, 70, 71, 74, 76, 77,
82; debate over in Maryland,
42–49; and democracy, 49, 70,
71; denial of, 36, 37, 38, 39, 40,
41, 42, 49, 52; English conception of, 4; English discovery
of, 21–22, 71; as foundation of
liberty and free government,
21, 22; as goal of American
Revolution, 1; in the houses
of representatives, 26; James
Madison on, 70; mistrust of,
28, 33; new concept of, 1, 49;
not embodying the American
people, 52, 75; postmodern
conception of, x; property
qualifications for, 13, 14; in
relation to government, 20;
and republics, 26; as "a species
of aristocracy," 50; and